2nd Edition

Understanding 1031
Tax-Free Exchanges

Thomas J. Mahlum, ABR, CRS, DREI, GRI

Dearborn
Real Estate Education

This publication is designed to provide accurate and authoritative information in regard to the subject matter covered. It is sold with the understanding that the publisher is not engaged in rendering legal, accounting, or other professional service. If legal advice or other expert assistance is required, the services of a competent professional should be sought.

President: Roy Lipner
Vice President, General Manager: Mehul Patel
Vice President of Product Development & Publishing: Evan M. Butterfield
Editorial Director: Kate DeVivo
Senior Development Editor: Anne Huston
Director of Production: Daniel Frey
Production Editor: Caitlin Ostrow
Production Artist: Caitlin Ostrow
Creative Director: Lucy Jenkins
Senior Product Manager: Melissa Kleeman

Published by Dearborn™ Real Estate Education
30 South Wacker Drive
Chicago, Illinois 60606-7481
(312) 836-4400
www.dearbornRE.com

Printed in the United States of America

08 09 10 9 8 7 6 5 4 3 2

In 1990 at a national Real Estate Educators Association conference in Florida, Vern Hoven, a CPA with a master's degree in taxation, gave a presentation on the new IRS rules on 1031 tax-free exchanges. Mr. Hoven predicted a huge increase in the use of the exchanges, noting that they would actually produce listings and sales once sellers, buyers, and agents became aware of these rules. If anything, Mr. Hoven was modest in his projections. Interest in and use of the 1031 tax-free exchange have grown beyond anyone's expectations. In 2003 taxpayers exchanged $175 billion, mostly in real estate.

This course is designed for real estate licensees as an introduction to the history, evolution, rules, and forms of Section 1031 of the Internal Revenue Code. The author is neither a CPA nor an attorney, but a practicing real estate broker who has studied and taught the topic of 1031 tax-free exchanges for the past 15 years. Many people have spent years executing and studying tax-free exchanges; this course covers the basics of the subject. The author has taken the liberty of simplifying the concepts and vocabulary. While he has changed the characters and particulars of some of the original stories relating to the history of 1031 exchanges, the basic concepts remain.

Although these exchanges have always been called "tax-free," the term is some-what of a misnomer. They are actually "tax-deferred" exchanges, also sometimes called "tax-delayed exchanges" and "like-kind exchanges." You will see the term "tax-free" used throughout this text; the term refers to a strategy used to defer the tax liability until some future date.

Most real estate professionals are neither CPAs nor attorneys; thus, providing tax advice is a violation of real estate licensing law as well as other state statutes. (In the perfect situation a meeting would be held between the real estate practitioner, his or her client, a CPA, and an attorney; together this group would develop a strategy for the successful completion of a tax-free exchange.) The only role of the real estate professional is to alert his or her seller/client to the existence of the IRS rules, show how they can be applied to a particular sale, and handle the real estate end of the transaction. All other functions must be performed by the CPA and/ or attorney. If a client does not have a CPA and/or attorney, the real estate pro-fessional should be prepared to recommend a professional who has the required skills and experience.

Your ability and willingness to discuss the tax ramifications of the impending sale, the possible benefits of owner financing, and the benefits of executing a 1031 tax-free exchange can set you apart from other real estate agents.

Thomas J. Mahlum, ABR, CRS, DREI, GRI, has been licensed as a broker in North Carolina since 1975 and has been studying the subject of tax-free exchanges for more than 30 years. He has taught prelicensing courses in North Carolina for 19 years, and for 15 years has been teaching real estate continuing education courses in North and South Carolina on a variety of subjects including tax-free exchanges. He currently teaches about 125 continuing education courses each year.

Mr. Mahlum has seen tremendous growth in interest in the subject of tax-free exchanges, as well as significant growth in the use of the exchanges in practice. This course was developed from Mr. Mahlum's work in the classroom.

In teaching the basics, Mr. Mahlum simplifies the concepts and vocabulary for practitioners who are familiarizing themselves with the new topic. He is cautious in advising students to work with attorneys and CPAs on a local level when executing 1031 tax-free exchanges.

Mr. Mahlum was formerly a principal in a real estate firm, and he continues to list and sell. He was the Property Management Broker for the Department of Veterans Affairs's homes in eight counties in North Carolina for 17 years. He is a member of the Jacksonville, North Carolina, Board of REALTORS®; the Real Estate Educators Association; and the North Carolina Real Estate Educators Association, from which he received the Real Estate Educator of the Year award in 2000.

Understanding 1031 Tax-Free Exchanges, 2nd Edition, would not have been possible without the thoughtful feedback of real estate practitioners and instructors. The author wishes to thank the following reviewers for their suggestions and contributions:

■ Richard J. Clemmer, Sr., D & D School of Real Estate, Johnson City, Tennessee

■ Bill Gallagher, DREI, GRI, ITI, President, Superior School of Real Estate, Charlotte, North Carolina

■ William Roos, EA, Master Tax Advisor, H&R Block, Minneapolis, Minnesota

The author also wishes to thank Sue Shearer for her extraordinary help in making this course possible. Sue has worked closely with the author for almost 20 years. The course development, its success in the classroom, and this book are all the result of Sue's editorial skills, patience, and insistence on clarity. Sue provided exceptional guidance throughout the entire project.

Finally, the author is indebted to Investors Title Exchange Corporation, Chapel Hill, North Carolina, for use of its forms in Chapter Five of this book, "The Paperwork."

General Discussion of Taxes

overview

The tax-free exchange, as it is commonly called, is really not "tax free." It is actually tax deferred. This means the tax that would normally be due on the disposition (sale) of the property is delayed or deferred until the future *if* the transaction conforms to the rules of Section 1031 of the Internal Revenue Code. In such an exchange (called a "1031") the property your client wants to sell is called the "old" property or the "relinquished" property. The property your client wants to purchase (exchange for) is called the "new" property, or the "replacement" property. Assuming that you and your client are executing a 1031 exchange, the term *sale* refers to the marketing of the relinquished property and the term *purchase* refers to the acquisition of the replacement property; together these equate to a successful 1031 exchange. Before moving on to a detailed discussion of the tax-free exchange, let's investigate where the tax liability originates. ■

learning objectives

Upon completing this chapter you will be able to:

■ describe the various types of taxes and the differences between earned income and unearned income;

■ identify the types of unearned income;

■ explain the differences between long-term and short-term capital gains;

■ explain the history of depreciation schedules;

■ calculate the capital gain on a real estate transaction; and

■ summarize the choices an investor client has upon the sale of investment property.

■ Income Taxes

A taxpayer is required to pay taxes on both ordinary/earned and unearned income.

- ■ **Taxes on Ordinary/Earned Income:** Taxes on ordinary/earned income are collected either through withholding by an employer or the taxpayer's payment of quarterly estimated taxes based on the previous year's income and deductions.

- ■ **Taxes on Unearned Income:** Four of the many types of unearned income that we will cover in this course are as follows:
    1. **Interest**—From all sources
    2. **Dividends**—From stock ownership
    3. **Rental**—Income after deductions for interest, taxes, expenses, and so forth
    4. **Capital Gains/Losses**—gains or losses resulting from the sale of a capital asset

What is the difference between ordinary/earned income and unearned income? *No Social Security or Medicare taxes are paid on unearned income.* Here is an example. Two taxpayers each earn $100,000 in 2008. Taxpayer A has a job; goes to work every day; pays expenses for work (transportation, clothing, lunch); and pays all federal, state, Social Security, and Medicare taxes. Taxpayer B earns $100,000, all as unearned income (interest/dividends/rental income and capital gains). *There is no Social Security or Medicare tax on unearned income.* Moreover, the capital gains tax is lower than the tax paid on earned income. Taxpayer B is at least 7.65 percent ahead of Taxpayer A, and even more so if Taxpayer A is self-employed. (Note that if all income for a lifetime is unearned there will be no Social Security benefits at retirement.)

■ Capital Gains Taxes

The tax law states that if you acquire (purchase, inherit, receive as a gift, and so forth) an asset and then sell the asset you may have either a capital gain (taxable) or a capital loss (possibly tax deductible). The following are examples of the sale of five assets. Four are personal property and one is real estate.

Car purchased for $500 (bill of sale is the proof)

- ■ Expenses $500 (receipts for parts as proof)
- ■ Sold for $2,000 minus $1,000 (initial purchase price plus expenses equals capital gain)
- ■ Pay federal and state income taxes on the $1,000 capital gain

Original Superman *comic book (mint condition): purchased for 5 cents by grandfather in 1935*

- ■ Handed down to grandchild (not inherited)
- ■ Sold last week for $65,000
- ■ Capital gain $64,999.95
- ■ Pay federal and state income taxes on the capital gain

Microsoft stock: You were at Harvard in the early 1980s and in your freshman year a fellow student/friend decided to quit college. You advised against that move. Your friend Bill asked to borrow $1,000 to fund a start-up company. You loaned him the money, and he gave you stock in his new company.

- You sell Microsoft stock in 2007 for a huge profit
- Capital gain
- Pay federal and state income taxes on the capital gain

Diamonds, gold, silver, jewelry, precious metals

- You frequent estate sales and buy jewelry, clean it up, and sell it later
- Capital gain
- Pay federal and state income taxes on the capital gain

Real estate: You bought many years ago (or perhaps just a few years ago) but the city has grown out to your property. There's a huge increase in value.

- You sell property
- Capital gain
- Pay federal and state income taxes on the capital gain

The reason taxes must be paid is that the property or item has been sold. If it is not sold, there is no tax liability. If the property or item is refinanced, there is no capital gain and no tax owed.

While this is not a course on the subject of inheritance, you should be aware that a client might be better off not selling (there goes the listing commission) his or her highly appreciated real estate, thereby incurring the capital gains tax. Currently the tax law allows the heirs to receive the first $2 million of a decedent's estate without paying any tax. This would be at the "stepped up" basis, which means the heirs' basis is the value of the property on the day the person died, not the basis carried by the dead person. In many cases the heirs are much better off inheriting the property than receiving it as a gift during the life of the grantor. The grantor would have diminished the value of the estate by giving the property to the family during his or her life rather than allowing them to receive the property upon the grantor's death. Agents should always refer their clients to a knowledgeable tax attorney in these matters.

There are *exceptions* to the capital gains law. One of these concerns *dealer* status.

Using the car example above, if you make a substantial amount of each year's income from buying, fixing up, and selling cars, you are considered a *dealer* in cars; the $1,000 profit you made is *not* capital gain income (15 percent maximum tax rate) but ordinary/earned income (35 percent maximum tax rate).

Caution! "Flipping" real estate (buying, fixing up, and selling within a short time period many times per year) would likely make you a dealer in the eyes of the IRS. (See one-year holding period discussed in Chapter Four.)

Long-Term versus Short-Term Capital Gains

The longer an investment is held before it is sold, the less the capital gains tax required. The government has changed the required time period over the years; presently, a gain on the sale of an investment held "more than one year" is treated as a long-term capital gain. If an asset is held one year or less and sold, the owner is taxed on the capital gain according to his or her tax bracket. The gain is treated as ordinary income and is referred to as a short-term capital gain. The taxes could be as high as 35 percent.

It is wise to keep assets for more than one year. As of 2006, the maximum tax rate* for long-term capital gains is 15 percent (5 percent for people who are in the two lowest tax brackets). "Boot," which will be discussed in Chapter Three, is a long-term capital gain.

*In 2011, capital gains rates will return to 2001 levels in the absence of any action by Congress.

■ Depreciation

Depreciation History

The possibility of depreciating improved real estate while the property is appreciating in value is a unique aspect of the U.S. tax laws. The ability to depreciate improved real estate has been a major motivation for investors to invest in real estate rather than alternative investment venues. The depreciation rules have changed over the years as shown below, and the real estate agent must be aware of the present rules and how they affect the investor's decision to invest.

- **Prior to 1981**—Residential real estate was depreciated on a 25-year to 40-year schedule.
- **1981 to 1986**—The Accelerated Cost Recovery System (ACRS) allowed a taxpayer to depreciate residential real estate in as little as 15 years at an accelerated (125 percent) declining balance. The ACRS created an enormous tax shelter for client/investors and made real estate a great investment. Bankers and stockbrokers were not happy. They felt real estate had an unfair advantage and lobbied Congress to change this.
- **1987 to present**—The Modified Accelerated Cost Recovery System (MACRS) extends depreciation over 27.5 years for residential real estate and 39 years for commercial real estate. Taxpayers may only use straight-line depreciation. All accelerated depreciation schedules have been eliminated.

Straight-Line Depreciation

Eliminating accelerated depreciation and increasing the depreciation time period in 1987 effectively halved the depreciation/tax shelter of any new real estate investment; bankers and stockbrokers win while investors and real estate agents lose. Only straight-line depreciation is allowed—that is, the same amount of depreciation must be taken each year. To calculate depreciation take the purchase price (cost) of the improved real estate and subtract the value of the land (land is not depreciable). Then divide by either 27.5 or 39 depending on whether the property is residential or commercial. The result is the amount of annual depreciation allowable.

Purchase price (may be different from present value) – Land/lot value (cannot depreciate land/dirt) = Depreciable asset value

When dealing with mixed-use (residential and commercial in the same building) property there is a rule that says if 80 percent or more of the income (not square footage) derived from a property is residential, then the entire building may be depreciated over 27.5 years. If the 80 percent rule is not met, the property is depreciated over 39 years. A good selling agent must be able to determine whether the past rental history and future rental projections will allow for at least 80 percent residential income, and therefore 27.5 years' depreciation—or that residential rental income is less than 80 percent, therefore requiring 39 years depreciation. This is crucial to the investor when considering the purchase.

■ Computing Capital Gain

While computing capital gain is a function of the tax preparer, it would be helpful for real estate agents to have some idea of the computation process. The following is a three-step process for computing the capital gain.

Step 1: Determining the cost basis of property

Original Cost Basis (Purchase Price)
+ Cost to Purchase*
+ Capital Improvements **
– Depreciation Taken (if any)
= Adjusted Cost Basis***

* This is an IRS term. Real estate agents call it "Buyer's Closing Costs." Not all buyer's closing costs that appear on page 2 of the HUD I (Uniform Settlement Statement) are deductible. For this example we are using all the buyer's closing costs.

** Improvements—This is a hotly debated subject between taxpayers and the IRS. To determine improvements tell your client to go back in his or her memory to the day the property was purchased. What is there now that was not there the day the property was purchased?

***The Adjusted Cost Basis may change from year to year.

Any of the following are examples of improvements: a new family room with fireplace, a bedroom or bath, new vinyl siding, paved driveway, a patio, a deck, paddle fans, a dishwasher, or fencing.

Routine maintenance is not an improvement. *Routine maintenance* means repairing or replacing something that was there when the property was purchased. If the property was an investment property when the fixing, repair, or replacement was accomplished, that cost was either taken as an expense in the year of repair or depreciated separately from the ongoing depreciation of the structure. On owner-occupied property, routine maintenance is NEVER deductible. The first rule of thumb—when in doubt, consult a CPA!

For example, questions could arise on the installation of a new heat pump that replaced an oil furnace. As the home had no previous air conditioning, clearly the cost of the heat pump with respect to the air conditioning is an improvement. Installation of ductwork is an improvement; nevertheless, the cost of a heat pump associated with replacing an existing heat system is probably not an improvement.

Upgrading of a roof from tin to asbestos shingles, for example, seems to indicate at least a partial improvement, as would a tile roof to replace an asphalt/fiberglass shingle roof. A client should talk to his or her CPA for guidance.

Adjusted Cost Basis

REALTOR® *George has two clients, Mr. Owner-Occupant and Mr. Investor, who want to sell their homes adjacent to each other. They bought their houses for the same price and at the same time. The only difference is that Mr. Investor has never lived in the home, and Mr. Occupant has lived in his property as his principal residence since purchasing it.*

	Mr. Owner-Occupant	Mr. Investor
Purchase Price	$30,000	$30,000
Cost to Purchase	- 0 -	- 0 -
Improvements	- 0 -	- 0 -
Depreciation	- 0 -	$25,000
Adjusted Cost Basis	$30,000	$ 5,000

In the previous example, closing costs and improvements were eliminated for simplicity.

The only difference in the adjusted cost basis for an owner-occupant versus an investor in this simplified example is the depreciation taken by the investor, which drops his adjusted cost basis to $5,000.

In the following example, the Adjusted Sales Price will be the same for Mr. Owner-Occupant and Mr. Investor.

Step 2:   Determining the Adjusted Sales Price

$ 110,000	Sales Price
– 10,000	Cost to Sell (most of seller's closing costs)
$ 100,000	Adjusted Sales Price

Step 3:   Computing Capital Gain

	Mr. Owner-Occupant	**Mr. Investor**
Adjusted Sales Price	$100,000	$100,000
Adjusted Cost Basis	–$30,000	–$5,000
Capital Gain	$ 70,000	$95,000

Mr. Owner-Occupant has a $70,000 capital gain and will pay no capital gain taxes. The Tax Reform Act of 1997 gave every taxpayer a $250,000 permanent exclusion of the capital gain on the sale of his or her principal residence. A husband and wife can take an exclusion of up to $500,000 if they file as "Married Filing Jointly (MFJ)." Note: This course is not intended to discuss the tax laws with respect to the sale of an owner-occupied home. More information on this topic can be found in *Real Estate and Taxes—What Every Agent Should Know*, also published by Dearborn™ Real Estate Education.

Now let's look at Mr. Investor. Mr. Investor has a total capital gain of $95,000. If he decides to pay taxes on this instead of the alternatives he will be taxed as follows:

■ $25,000 (depreciated capital gain) will be taxed at 25 percent.

■ $70,000 (appreciated capital gain) will be taxed for most taxpayers at 15 percent (taxpayers in the lowest tax brackets would pay 5 percent capital gains tax).

■ Recapturing Depreciation

In 1997 the maximum capital gain tax rate dropped from 28 percent to 20 percent. However, if depreciation was previously taken, that amount is taxed at either 15 or 25 percent. For the purposes of this introductory course, 25 percent will be used. This is known as *recapture*. In effect the government is recapturing some of the tax savings the taxpayer accumulated over the years the property was depreciated. The taxpayer needs to break down the capital gain into two parts—calculating the depreciated capital gain (the amount of depreciation taken during the period of ownership) and calculating the appreciated capital gain (the amount the property went up in value during ownership). An example follows.

Capital Gains/Depreciation		
$	100,000	Property purchase price
+	3,000	Closing expenses (buyer closing costs)
–	28,000	Depreciation taken ten years
	75,000	Adjusted cost basis
	300,000	Sales price
–	20,000	Cost to sell (seller closing costs)
	280,000	Adjusted sales price
–	75,000	Adjusted cost basis
$	205,000	Total capital gain

The total capital gain is $205,000. Part of it ($28,000) is *depreciated* capital gain and will be taxed at 25 percent. The remainder, $177,000 ($205,000 – $28,000 depreciation), is the *appreciated* capital gain, which will be taxed at a maximum of 15 percent (the cost basis is not taxed).

Figure 1.1 is a form that can be used as part of a listing agent's presentation to a seller. This form and its use should be approved by your managing broker before presenting it to a seller. Many agents find that its use has enhanced their listing presentation. The seller deserves to know the tax consequences of the sale of the property at the time of the listing and not be surprised by huge tax liabilities come April 15th. In a perfect world the seller would have discussed the sale of the property with his or her tax preparer, but few do this until it is time to prepare their tax return. By that time it is too late to accomplish an installment sale (discussed in Chapter Two) or a tax-free exchange (discussed in Chapters Three through Five). Sellers appreciate the efforts of a listing agent who brings to their attention the tax implications of the sale of their real estate property.

After a little practice with Figure 1.1 you will be comfortable using it in your listing presentations. Work through the example in Figure 1.1, especially the bottom section where the approximate tax liability is calculated. Remember that this exercise does not have to be perfectly accurate; it is an approximation. Using your own residence for practice, work your way through this form on the lines provided.

Figure 1.1 | Computing the Capital Gain and Tax Due

	EXAMPLE	YOUR FIGURES
Step 1:		
Original Cost Basis (purchase price)	$100,000	$ _250,000_
+ Cost to Purchase (closing costs)	2,000	$ _5,000_
+ Capital Improvements	20,000	$ _115,000_
− Depreciation Taken (if any)	14,000	$ _____
= Adjusted Cost Basis	$108,000	$ _265,000_
		_415,370-_
Step 2:		
Actual Sales Price	$324,000	$ _959,000_
− Cost to Sell (closing costs)	28,000	$ _30,000_
= Adjusted Sales Price	$296,000	$ _929,000_
Step 3:		
Adjusted Sales Price	$296,000	$ _929,000_
− Adjusted Cost Basis	108,000	$ _415,000_ _370,000_
= Capital Gain (or Loss)	$188,000	$ _514,000_ _559,000_
COMPUTING CAPITAL GAIN TAX		
Total Capital Gain (1)	$188,000	$ _____
− Depreciation Taken (2)	14,000	$ _____
= Appreciated Capital Gain (3)	$174,000	$ _____
Appreciated Capital Gain × 15% = (4)	$26,100	$ _____
− Depreciation Taken × 25% = (5)	3,500	$ _____
Capital Gain Tax Due = (4) + (5)	$29,600	$ _____ _478,000_

This is not an IRS form and should not be submitted to the IRS. The "Tax Due" is only an approximation of the tax due on the sale of the property. The actual "Tax Due" may be higher or lower depending on the balance of your tax return. It is strongly suggested that you seek the advice of a tax professional to determine an estimated tax due based on all your income and deductions. Estimated tax payments may be necessary to avoid underpayment penalties.

case study

PDQ Realty is a small real estate investment company in St. Paul, Minnesota. Six months ago the company purchased an abandoned house and lot at 427 Viking Way for $250,000 plus $5,000 in closing costs. PDQ has been contacted by the Golden Gopher retirement home, located across the street from PDQ's property. Golden Gopher would like to purchase the entire parcel to build a small parking garage for its staff and residents.

PDQ is anxious to sell; they contract with real estate broker Terry Fischetti to handle the transaction. PDQ wants Terry to advise them on setting a sales price that will provide maximum profit with minimal taxes. Terry suggests that PDQ reject Golden Gopher's offer, make capital improvements to the property, rent it for several years, and then sell the property at the fair market value at that time.

1. Terry most likely suggested PDQ reject Golden Gopher's offer because
   a. gain on the immediate sale of 427 Viking Way would be taxed as capital gain income rather than earned income.
   b. IRS regulations penalize the sale of property that is not used for "like kind" purposes.
   c. "flipping" real estate is illegal in most states.
   d. gain on the immediate sale of 427 Viking Way would be taxed as a short-term capital gain, rather than as a long-term capital gain.

2. PDQ follows Terry's advice and decides to rent 427 Viking Way for several years after making capital improvements totaling $115,000. Assuming an eventual sales price of $959,000 and that PDQ takes no depreciation and would need to pay $30,000 in closing costs to sell, what is the amount of the capital gain?
   a. $559,000
   b. $564,000
   c. $589,000
   d. $594,000

Student Comments

Please provide your comments regarding the basic principle(s) addressed in this case study, and its relevance to the subject matter:

_____

_____

_____

◼ Conclusion

We have seen how the various types of income are taxed and how capital gains are calculated. Now that we have seen the tax consequences of the sale of a capital asset, we will use the example of Mr. Owner-Occupant and Mr. Investor to discuss alternative strategies to spread out the tax liability through the use of an installment sale (Chapter Two) or a tax-free exchange (Chapters Three through Five).

■ Chapter One Review Questions

1. The property that a taxpayer has owned for some time and wants to sell as part of a Section 1031 tax-free exchange is what type of property?

    a. Replacement
    b. Depreciated
    c. Severed
    d. Relinquished

2. Capital gain income is

    a. not taxed.
    b. taxed higher than ordinary income.
    c. taxed lower than ordinary income.
    d. taxed and includes Social Security income taxes.

3. The property that a taxpayer wants to acquire as part of a Section 1031 tax-free exchange is called

    a. replacement property.
    b. depreciated property.
    c. severed property.
    d. relinquished property.

4. Mr. North sold a property that had an adjusted cost basis of $237,000 and an adjusted sales price of $1,487,500. How much is the capital gain?

    a. $1,250,500
    b. $1,724,500
    c. $987,500
    d. $1,687,000

5. Client Smith purchased a property for $205,000. He has taken $83,000 depreciation over the past few years. His closing costs to purchase the property were $9,000. What was Client Smith's adjusted cost basis for the property?

    a. $214,000
    b. $131,000
    c. $340,000
    d. $284,000

6. If Client Smith sold the property for $487,000 and had $37,000 in closing expenses, what was his adjusted sales price?

    a. $450,000
    b. $408,000
    c. $524,000
    d. $487,000

7. If Client Herbold has an adjusted sales price of $872,000 and an adjusted cost basis of $146,500, what is the amount of the capital gain?

    a. $429,000
    b. $687,500
    c. $725,500
    d. $1,018,500

8. Taxpayer B.J. (33 percent tax bracket) has a capital gain of $478,000 on an improved property that she has depreciated in the amount of $146,000. What is her gross tax liability?

    a. $86,300
    b. $103,900
    c. $119,500
    d. $112,200

9. Taxpayer A. P. Hill (35 percent tax bracket) sold property with capital gains of $854,000. He had taken depreciation of $206,000. How much tax does Mr. Hill owe based only on the recapture of the depreciation?

    a. $170,800
    b. $213,500
    c. $129,600
    d. $51,500

10. How much total tax does Mr. Hill (question 9) owe on his property?

    a. $180,100
    b. $213,500
    c. $148,700
    d. $129,600

Installment Sales

Now that we have determined the amount of capital gain our investor in Chapter One is facing, we want to be able to present him with alternatives. Should he bite the bullet and pay the tax (never a good alternative); sell the property by executing an installment sale (owner financing); or execute a 1031 tax-free exchange? In this chapter we will consider the installment sale alternative. ■

learning objectives

Upon completing this chapter you will be able to:

■ summarize the choices an investor client has upon the sale of his or her investment property;

■ describe a typical installment sale situation;

■ list and explain the benefits of an installment sale to the buyer, seller, and agent; and

■ list and explain the potential disadvantages of an installment sale to the buyer, seller, and agent.

■ What Is an Installment Sale?

An installment sale takes place when the seller (through his or her real estate listing agent) offers to sell the property by taking back owner/seller financing. The buyer does not arrange financing through a bank or mortgage lender. In effect, the seller is the bank or lender. For many properties, an installment sale is the "best" method of sale. Installment sales can be used for vacant land or improved real estate.

Most agents do not discuss the possibility of their seller/client's taking back seller financing (installment sale) as a marketing tool in the sale of investment property. This could be a mistake from the agent's standpoint. Owner financing may appeal to a buyer and cause the property to be sold more quickly. An agent has not exercised *skill, care, and diligence* (one of the basic duties an agent owes to his or her client) if the agent fails to discuss the installment sale and the 1031 tax-free exchange as alternatives. Why do the agents fail to discuss this subject during their listing presentation? It is probably a result of a general lack of knowledge of the benefits and drawbacks of the installment sale, which are presented in this chapter.

There are many ways to structure an installment sale (contract for deed, purchase money deed of trust, installment land contract). Consult your broker or attorney for particulars.

Installment Sale

Suppose we have a buyer for the $110,000 property in Chapter One. Instead of the buyer arranging a new loan, the selling agent suggests an offer to purchase wherein the seller takes back owner financing. The buyer puts down $30,000 and the seller takes back an $80,000 mortgage at a negotiated interest of 8 percent and for a term of 15 years (180 monthly payments). All terms of the sale are negotiable between the buyer and seller.

■ Advantages of an Installment Sale

Advantages of an installment sale to the buyer(s) include:

- Low closing costs—There is no loan origination fee, credit report, or discount points. There are some closing costs, which are optional but should be recommended by an agent, such as a survey, title search, title insurance, and home inspection.
- Fast closing—There is no waiting period for mortgage approval. Closings can take place in days, not weeks.

The advantages to the seller(s) include:

- Fast closing, for this type of sale gets the property off the market, and the seller receives some of the proceeds in just a few days
- Creation of an annuity for the seller and heirs
- Future property taxes paid by buyer(s)
- Buyer purchases homeowner insurance policy showing the seller as first mortgagee
- Buyer responsible for all future maintenance
- Seller collects negotiated interest rate instead of depositing sales proceeds in a bank at a lower interest rate
- This type of sale spreads the capital gains tax over the 15 years. Taxes are paid only on the portion of the capital gain received in each year. The total payments are broken down and taxes paid as follows:
  1. Interest: Federal and state taxes, no Social Security or Medicare
  2. Cost basis portion: No tax
  3. Depreciated capital gain: 25 percent—could be as low as 15 percent (recapture)
  4. Appreciated capital gain: 15 percent maximum (could be as low as 5 percent)

- Seller in a lower tax bracket at retirement would pay even less taxes on the interest portion of the installment payments
- Installment sale often used when the residential property needs repairs and does not qualify for VA/FHA financing

Disadvantages of Installment Sales

There are a number of potential disadvantages of installment sales. Once you explain them, your seller can decide if the advantages outweigh the disadvantages.

What If Buyer Defaults?

If buyer defaults, foreclosure is the seller's remedy. Foreclosure costs some money for an attorney and takes some time. Fortunately, the probability of this is low.

- Since 1948, of all FHA loans in the United States, approximately 6.5 percent have been foreclosed.
- Since 1947, of all VA loans in the United States approximately 5.5 percent have been foreclosed (1997–98–99 fiscal year report says that the foreclosure rate is at 4 percent).
- Since record keeping began on conventional loans, approximately 3.5 percent have been foreclosed.

Nationally, approximately 4 percent of all loans end up in foreclosure. That means 96 percent of all mortgages are paid. Recent publicity about subprime mortgages would suggest some slight variation in the foreclosure rate for all mortgages. What, then, is the probability of foreclosure when the buyer puts down $30,000 on the purchase of a $110,000 property? Extremely low! What if $15,000 down? What if $5,000 down? Obviously, the smaller the down payment, the greater the risk of foreclosure.

Why are approximately 4 percent of all mortgages foreclosed? Each loan applicant had to qualify to obtain loan approval. But something happened to the buyer after loan approval and closing that caused their lives to change for the worse. Divorce is the single leading cause of foreclosure; the second is job related (closing down the factory); and the third is health related. Approximately 27 percent of Americans have no major medical coverage. A major illness to parents or children can result in hundreds of thousand of dollars in medical/hospital expenses. Often loss of the home is an additional tragedy in their life.

When buyers are in this situation, they shouldn't let the mortgage go into foreclosure. There are other options—rent out the property and use the rent to pay the mortgage, for example. Selling the house, even at a loss, is better than losing everything. What do buyers lose? The $30,000 down payment plus the closing costs paid to purchase, payments made thus far, and any money spent to fix up the property. Give this advice to buyers at closing. Suggest they call the real estate agent before the situation gets out of hand.

If against all odds the buyer does go into default, foreclosure is inevitable. After foreclosure the question is, "Is the buyer still in possession?" If so, action for eviction is necessary. The next issue is the condition of the property. Repairs may be required before a client can rent or sell the property.

Prepayment

Prepayment is another possible disadvantage. If the buyer inherits a substantial amount of money or wins the lottery and pays off the loan, the seller/client will have to pay all capital gains taxes due in the year of receipt of the funds. This means all the work involved in creating the owner financing just went down the tubes. May the client stop the buyer from prepaying the loan? No. Can the client do anything to discourage the buyer from prepaying the loan? Yes. A prepayment penalty can be included in the loan documents. This prepayment penalty is due if the buyer prepays the loan. While the prepayment penalty does not cover the tax liability it helps a little. *Caution:* In many states a prepayment penalty is not allowed for certain mortgages in certain situations. Always check your state law.

Bankruptcy

If bankruptcy by the buyer becomes a problem, action must be taken in a timely manner to take the mortgage debt out of the bankruptcy proceedings. A client should see an attorney if the buyer files for bankruptcy. The client must be on the alert for this possibility as well as demanding prompt proof of annual payments of taxes and receipt of a copy of the insurance policy each year. There are downsides to everything. But the real estate professional should make the seller/client aware of the benefits and possible drawbacks of this marketing idea.

NOTE: The IRS allocates the payment received on an installment note as being first, interest, and second, principal. The principal is further allocated—first as the depreciation taken (depreciated capital gain) taxed at 15 percent/25 percent (recapture) *until it is paid in full,* and then as appreciated capital gain, taxed at a maximum of 15 percent. The portion of payments that is the taxpayer's cost basis is not taxed at all.

> *Mrs. Smuckatelli received 12 equal installment payments of $872 in 2003 (the year of the sale). She reports $10,464, of which $2,852 is interest. She will report the interest as "interest income" and pay taxes according to whatever tax bracket she is in. The balance of the payments—$7,612—is principal on the promissory note. Assuming Mrs. Smuckatelli took considerable depreciation during her years of ownership, all the $7,612 is depreciated capital gain and would be taxed at 15/25 percent.*

case study

Moira Tennenbaum wants to sell Happy Dell, an investment property she owns outside Darien, Connecticut. Moira lives in Darien but is preparing to retire to Branson, Missouri. She is anxious to sell Happy Dell quickly, and tells her real estate broker, Sandy Tyson, to find a buyer as quickly as possible. Within a week Sandy tells Moira that they have a potential buyer—the Nelsons.

However, the Nelsons do not think they can get a mortgage at the current asking price for Happy Dell. Moira tells Sandy to lower the price. Sandy tells Moira there might be a way to conduct the transaction immediately and still get the asking price—an installment sale. Moira has never heard of this kind of transaction, and wants to know how it works before she agrees to consider it. She particularly is concerned about tax consequences.

1. Which of the following would NOT be true of an installment sale?
    a. Moira finances the sale.
    b. The sale creates an annuity for Moira.
    c. Moira would pay for future maintenance and repairs.
    d. The closing is comparatively quick and cheap.

2. What are the tax consequences for Moira?
    a. She pays future property taxes.
    b. She does not pay capital gains tax.
    c. Installment payments are taxed at Moira's income tax bracket.
    d. Her capital gains tax is spread out over the term of the seller financing.

Student Comments

Please provide your comments regarding the basic principle(s) addressed in this case study, and its relevance to the subject matter:

_____

_____

_____

■ Conclusion

The installment sale is a widely ignored vehicle for the marketing of real estate due to the lack of knowledge by real estate licensees of the advantages and disadvantages of this financing alternative. If your client is unwilling or unable to consider this vehicle, the following chapters may present a solution to your client's tax problem.

■ Chapter Two Review Questions

1. In an installment sale (owner financing) the seller is responsible for maintenance of the property after closing.

   a. True

   b. False *(circled)*

2. There are no risks involved for our seller/client in executing an installment sale.

   a. True

   b. False *(circled)*

3. In an installment sale (owner financing) the seller and buyer negotiate the terms of financing, such as interest rate and time period.

   a. True *(circled)*

   b. False

4. In an installment sale the disadvantage is the long time it takes to close the sale.

   a. True

   b. False *(circled)*

5. Mr. Yadlowski (35 percent tax bracket) expects a capital gain on the sale of unimproved investment property of $135,000. Assume he arranges an installment sale with no closing costs and he receives $45,000 cash at closing (December 31). How much federal capital gains tax did Mr. Yadlowski avoid paying in the year of sale?

   a. $9,000

   b. $13,500 *(circled)*

   c. $27,000

   d. $36,000

   handwritten: 90,000 ×.15 45,0000 90000 1350.00

6. Which portion of an installment payment is not taxed?

   a. Appreciated capital gain

   b. Depreciated capital gain

   c. Interest

   d. Cost basis *(circled)*

7. Which portion of an installment payment is taxed at 15/25 percent?

   a. Appreciated capital gain

   b. Depreciated capital gain *(circled)*

   c. Interest

   d. Cost basis

8. Which portion of an installment payment is taxed at the taxpayer's income tax bracket?

   a. Appreciated capital gain

   b. Depreciated capital gain

   c. Interest *(circled)*

   d. Cost basis

9. Which portion of an installment payment is taxed at 15 percent?

   a. Appreciated capital gain *(circled)*

   b. Depreciated capital gain

   c. Interest

   d. Cost basis

10. Mr. Goldsmith (35 percent tax bracket) sold investment property in 2006 on an installment sale to Miss Lightfoot. The monthly payments of principal and interest are $1,200. In the year 2007 the interest portion is $3,800. Assuming that the balance of the payment is depreciated capital gains, how much capital gains tax does Mr. Goldsmith owe?

    a. $3,050

    b. $3,600

    c. $2,880

    d. $1,590 *(circled)*

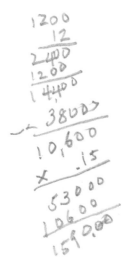

handwritten: 1200 ×12 2400 1200 14400 −3800 10,600 ×.15 53000 10600 1590.00

The 1031 Tax-Free Exchange

overview

If the installment sale is not a viable alternative for the taxpayer, possibly the Section 1031 tax-free exchange will solve the taxpayer's problem. In this chapter we will see how the exchange has evolved from a simple trade of properties requiring two willing and able parties to the presently more common multiparty exchange. ■

learning objectives

Upon completing this chapter you will be able to:

■ list the major historical events that affected the use of 1031 exchanges;

■ identify the major provisions of the law;

■ list the four classes of real estate as per IRS;

■ understand a basic/straight/simultaneous exchange;

■ explain the concept of "boot";

■ explain the concepts of "buy up," "mortgage up," and "spend all the money"; and

■ describe the role Starker played in the evolution of the exchange, including the reverse Starker exchange.

■ What Is a Tax-Free Exchange?

As defined in Chapter One, a tax-free exchange is a method of selling a capital asset, like real estate, according to certain prescribed rules and procedures in such a manner that all or most of the capital gains taxes will be deferred to the future. It may help to think that the taxpayer is not selling a capital asset but is reorganizing his or her investments. Congress decided this reorganization was not a taxable event if conducted in accordance with certain rules.

■ History/Evolution of the Tax-Free Exchange

Anyone familiar with tax-free exchanges of 20 or more years ago is amazed at the number and simplicity of exchanges being performed today. The history of tax-free exchanges dates back to the 1920s.

- ■ 1921–28—The first tax-free exchanges were executed. (This is not a new concept: it has just improved over time.) These exchanges involved two parties who traded/swapped properties.
- ■ 1954—Congress passed Section 1031 of the Internal Revenue Code, giving the name to 1031. This was a rewrite or codification/reorganization of all the laws affecting exchanges, including court decisions on this subject.

The pertinent wording of the law follows. The italicized words will be discussed in greater detail here and in Chapter Four.

No gain or loss shall be recognized [in other words, no taxes have to be paid and no losses can be taken at the time of the exchange] on the exchange of property *held* for *productive use in trade or business,* or for investment, if such property is exchanged solely for property of *like kind* which is to be *held* for *productive use in trade or business* or *for investment.*" (Section 1031 Internal Revenue Code)

■ Why Would a Client Want to Exchange?

The following is a list of possible reasons why your client may want to exchange:

1. The client is determined to sell for some/any reason (age of neighborhood or maintenance expenses or whatever).
2. The client is tired of residential rentals and wants commercial or vacant land.
3. The client wants to switch into faster-appreciating investments.
4. The client wants to get rid of appreciated non-income-producing vacant land and buy income-producing investments.
5. Federal and state capital gain taxes can exceed 22 percent on the capital gain.
6. The client sells fully depreciated property and buys a more valuable property, thus creating a new tax shelter.
7. The client wants to leverage up his or her investments.
8. The client wants to defer payment of tax liability to take advantage of the "time value of money."
9. The client wants to rearrange his or her holdings in anticipation of death.
10. The client mistakenly thinks that selling is the only way to secure much needed cash.
11. The client wants his or her investment property to be near his or her principal residence.

■ IRS Classifies Real Estate

The IRS has classified all real estate as follows:

1. Principal residence (Including second homes and time-shares)
   Example: Second homes are properties used by taxpayer's family, usually

not rented out to others. Time-shares are personal use property sometimes traded in for personal use of someone else's time-share (swapping).

2. Property held for the productive use in trade or business
   Example: Many different types of entities may own property for trade or business, for example, single persons, a husband and wife, partnerships, limited liability companies, corporations, and trusts.

3. Investment property
   Example: Most agents' clients fall into this category. Investment property also may be owned by single persons, a husband and wife, partnerships, limited liability companies, corporations, and trusts. An investment of 200 acres of land, a lot at the beach, an apartment complex, a single-family home, or an industrial building are all examples of investment properties.

4. Inventory property held primarily for sale
   Example: A dealer/developer purchases 100 acres and builds 200 new homes. This is his inventory. The owner is considered a dealer in real estate; a dealer is someone who makes his or her living (substantial portion of income) from a certain activity, in this case the development of real estate. The property is classified as inventory.

5. A dealer is not prohibited from doing a 1031 exchange by virtue of being a dealer/developer. He or she is only prohibited from doing an exchange on any of his or her inventory property.

Summary: On What Properties Are 1031 Tax-Free Exchanges Allowed?

Tax-free exchanges ARE allowed by the IRS on:

■ Property held for the productive use in trade or business

■ Investment property

Tax-free exchanges ARE NOT allowed by the IRS on:

■ Personal residences, second homes, and time-shares purchased for personal use

■ Inventory property

What May Be Exchanged?

Other examples can be even more complicated. Take, for example, a convenience store such as a 7-Eleven or a Circle K store.

■ May a tax-free exchange be executed on the land and building? *(Yes)*

■ May a tax-free exchange be executed on personal property such as the cash register, coolers, refrigerators, and so on? *(Yes)**

■ May a tax-free exchange be executed on the bread-milk-tobacco products? *(No, those items are inventory property)* **

* Personal property held for the productive use in trade or business
**Inventory property held for sale

Ineligible Property

The following items are not eligible for a 1031 tax-free exchange as either the relinquished or replacement property:

1. Personal residence (principal residence)
2. Second home
3. Retirement home
4. Inventory property
5. Time-shares purchased for personal use
6. Stocks, bonds, or notes
7. Securities or other evidence of indebtedness
8. Stock in trade or property held primarily for sale (inventory)
9. Partnership interests
10. Chooses in action (the right to receive money or other personal property as a result of court action)
11. Certificates of trust

■ Things You Should Know about Tax-Free Exchanges

The Simultaneous Exchange

This basic type of 1031 tax-free exchange is also known as a "straight exchange," "simple exchange," or "simultaneous exchange." It can best be described in the following example.

Client Peter owns an investment property (Property A) in Charlotte, North Carolina, worth $100,000. He has taken a lot of depreciation, and the property has appreciated greatly. His equity is $50,000 with an assumable loan. He wants to sell the property, but is looking at a large tax liability. He wants to purchase investment property in Phoenix, Arizona.

Client Paul owns an investment property (Property B) in Phoenix, Arizona, worth $120,000. His assumable mortgage balance is $80,000. He has $40,000 in equity. Paul has taken considerable depreciation and the property has gone up in value, but he wants to sell and buy investment property in Charlotte, North Carolina, where his daughter, Beth, is attending UNC-Charlotte.

This is a perfect opportunity for an exchange. The clients view each other's property and are ready to close.

Wait a minute. It may appear that Paul is getting ripped off on this deal. He is trading his $120,000 property for Peter's $100,000 property. Wrong! The first lesson is that tax-free exchanges are not executed based upon the "value of the property." They are executed based on the equity. In this case Peter is actually losing, not Paul. Peter is giving $50,000 equity and only receiving $40,000 equity—and Peter says "no deal" unless the deal is fair and equal. Thus, Paul must give $40,000 equity and come up with an additional $10,000. It could be a parcel of real estate worth $10,000. It could be a $10,000 car. It could be $10,000 in stock. It could be anything given in exchange, and if it is not real estate it is called "unlike kind" property. In fact, it is usually paid in cash and has another name, "boot." The basic rule is that "boot" is taxable to the recipient. It may be partially offset by deductible closing costs.

Now let's look at Peter and Paul as a CPA would look at the transaction to determine liability, if any. Peter and Paul need to know this information before they sign any real estate contracts.

Peter (Property A Charlotte)		Paul (Property B Phoenix)	
Value	$100,000	Value	$120,000
Mortgage Balance	$50,000	Mortgage Balance	$80,000
Equity	$50,000	Equity	$40,000
		Cash boot	$10,000

The $10,000 from Paul would have to be supplemented with about $7,000 needed to cover the real estate sales commission and other seller's closing costs associated with the sale of his property in Phoenix, as well as the buyer's closing costs associated with his purchase of the Charlotte property.

Peter needs to understand that he will only receive about $3,000 of the $10,000, for he also owes a commission, the seller's normal closing costs associated with the sale of the Charlotte property, and the buyer's closing costs associated with his purchase of the Phoenix property.

Each of these investors has some tax liability based on the exchange just outlined. Again we are continuing to look at this as a CPA would. For simplicity, the following examples exclude closing costs.

*Peter will have to report the receipt of "boot" in the year received. Thus this exchange is not a 100 percent tax-free exchange. It is about 90 percent tax free and 10 percent taxable. This is called a "partial exchange," and these are perfectly legal. **The exchange does not have to be 100 percent tax-free to be legal.***

Peter (Property A Charlotte)

Relieved of mortgage	$ 50,000
Assumes/Creates mortgage	$ 80,000
	($30,000)

This figure will factor into the cost basis of new property B

Boot cash	$10,000

$10,000 capital gain income*

*Must pay taxes in the year of the exchange.

Now that we have discussed Peter's situation, let's look at Paul's. (This example also excludes closing costs to keep it simple.)

Paul (Property B Phoenix)

Relieved of mortgage	$80,000
Assumes/Creates mortgage	$50,000
	+ $30,000
Boot cash	$10,000
Net boot	$20,000*

*Must report $20,000 in boot capital gain and pay tax in the year of the exchange.

Paul has a net boot of $20,000, taxable to him in the year of the exchange. This exchange turns out to be about 85 percent tax free and about 15 percent taxable.

The lesson here is that all mortgages have to be factored into the equation. If a mortgage is paid off on the sale of a relinquished property but not replaced as a mortgage on the replacement property, tax liability will result (this is an example of "boot").

100 Percent Tax-Free Exchange

If you want the deal to be totally tax free you need to

- buy up;
- mortgage up; and
- spend all the money.

If you purchase a replacement property more expensive than the sales price of the relinquished property, *and* end up with at least as big a mortgage on the replacement property as you had on the relinquished property, *and* spend all the money (proceeds of sale) that came out of the relinquished property, there will be NO TAX LIABILTY.

Caution: The IRS has a rule that says in the case of a "multiple exchange" (where more than one property is the replacement property) the taxpayer must break the replacement properties into "exchange groups." This is a complicated mathematical formula prorating the cost basis of the relinquished properties among the multiple replacement properties, and the result could cause some tax liability at this time even though the taxpayer has followed our advice to "buy up, mortgage up, and spend all the money." As always, have your client consult with his or her CPA.

Another Scenario

Let's look at another scenario involving our friends Peter and Paul. Peter still wants to sell the Charlotte investment property and Paul wants to buy it to live in with his family. Paul does not own any real estate in Phoenix, so it appears that no 1031 exchange is possible.

However, a clever real estate agent can suggest the following idea. Peter has located a motel property in Phoenix that he wants to own. Peter asks Paul to go to Phoenix and purchase the motel property. After the closing in Phoenix, Peter will exchange (swap/trade) the Charlotte property for the Phoenix property Paul has just purchased.

This is perfectly legal and brings up the lesson that the real estate transaction does not have to be a tax-free exchange for *both* parties. Sometimes it is an exchange for only one of the parties (in this case, Peter). Paul has no prior ownership of real estate and has no tax problem as he will be exchanging the Phoenix property for no profit, therefore no capital gain.

As a practical matter, unless Paul is a very sophisticated investor he will not be willing to travel to Phoenix and purchase a property he does NOT want to own in order to put him in a position to trade it to Peter for a property in Charlotte he does want to own. Real estate agents in the past found that doing tax-free exchanges was difficult if not impossible. It would be unbelievable luck to find two investors who desired to exchange properties. It was especially difficult for properties in different cities and/or states. The following section on the Starker exchange helps to show why.

T. J. Starker Challenges the IRS

By far the most dramatic series of events affecting the evolution of Section 1031 law resulted from the battles between the IRS and Mr. Thomas J. Starker. The following discussion of events is intended to show the reader the result of Starker's activities. The actual details and names in the Starker story have been changed. For this course, the author wants the reader to understand the concept of Starker's actions and the historic impact those actions had on future tax laws.

Mr. Starker was a wealthy owner of real estate living in the northwestern area of the United States during the 1960s with real estate holdings in various states. He was approached by a woman named Mary T., a potential purchaser of 100 acres of land in Oregon on which she hoped to build a home and raise her family. While the offering price of $100,000 was very attractive, Starker was reluctant to sell because of high capital gains taxes. He proposed an exchange but Mary T. only owned property in the eastern United States, and Starker was not interested.

Shortly thereafter some land in Walla Walla, Washington, came on the market. Starker had wanted this land for years and could have paid cash. Nevertheless, Starker called Mary T. and asked her to go to Walla Walla, purchase the land, and afterward exchange the Walla Walla property for the Oregon property. Mary T. refused. Starker discontinued negotiations at that point but was still determined to make it work. He finally came up with an idea that would change 1031 forever. He called Mary T. and asked her if she still wanted the 100 acres for $100,000. She said yes. Starker again proposed she buy the Walla Walla property and exchange it for the Oregon property. Again she said no. Starker agreed to sell her the 100 acres for $100,000 (certified funds) with the closing to be the following Friday at noon at his attorney's office. On Friday morning Starker flew to Walla Walla.

At 1:00 PM he called his attorney to see if Mary T. had showed up with the $100,000. She had, and that part of the deal was closed. The $100,000 was put in "safe harbor" (the concept of safe harbor/qualified intermediary is discussed later, but it is *very* important that Starker did not touch the money). Starker then negotiated to buy the Walla Walla land and contracted at $105,000 to close within 30 days. At closing Starker used the $100,000 from the "safe harbor" (Mary T.'s money from the sale of Oregon property) and $5,000 of his money to purchase the Walla Walla property.

When Starker filed his 1040 income tax return the IRS took one look at the above transaction and said that it was not a 1031 exchange because Mary T. never purchased (took title) to the Walla Walla property prior to exchanging with Starker. Starker argued that it was a 1031 because Mary T. got the Oregon land, the seller in Walla Walla got $100,000 plus $5,000 from him, and he secured the Walla Walla property deed. This issue went through the tax courts for eight years and finally Starker won.

Then Starker executed a similar deal, with a slightly different twist. This case also went to court and after two years Starker won. Then he did it a third time, again just slightly differently, went back to the courts, and after two years Starker won again. In each of these cases the IRS disallowed the 1031 exchange and Starker had to fight it out in tax court.

This established the concept of a deferred exchange, also called the Starker deferred exchange. The Starker is a *three-party exchange,* while the basic *simultaneous exchange* is a two-party exchange. Now a taxpayer did not have to find a willing owner of replacement property who also wanted the taxpayer's relinquished property. We cannot overemphasize the importance of these court cases and the collective impact these cases had on the evolution of exchanges. Starker is famous because of his 1031-related activities.

Reverse Starker Exchange

The *Starker v. IRS* cases described earlier spanned a period of more than 15 years. Some time later Starker executed another transaction that resulted in great notoriety, but for the strangest of reasons. Again the particulars have been changed in the following example but they are designed to present the concept of the reverse Starker exchange. As you will learn, the effect on 1031 exchanges was dramatic.

Another property, in Beaverton, Oregon, came on the market. Starker wanted it badly and could have paid cash. But he decided to try an exchange. He called his old friend Mary T. and asked her if she would consider buying another 100 acres, this time for $200,000, adjacent to her existing 100-acre property. She said yes, but that the sale could not be closed for 120 days. That was unacceptable, because by then the desired property in Beaverton would be gone. Starker wrestled with this dilemma and came up with this solution.

Starker entered into a contract to sell Mary T. the 100 Oregon acres for $200,000 with a closing date of 120 days in the future. He then entered into a contract to purchase the Beaverton property, but the seller insisted on closing in 30 days. All logic, common sense, and IRS rules said a taxpayer had to sell the relinquished property, then buy the replacement property. Starker went ahead with the sales and later filed his 1040 tax return showing the sales as qualifying for 1031 treatment. What do you think the IRS did? The answer is nothing!

The IRS chose to do nothing. They chose to ignore what Starker had done—*to not disallow* the so-called tax-free exchange. Did the IRS feel it was a qualifying 1031? No. The IRS ignored it and said nothing, because if they disallowed it, they would end up in tax court, and should Starker win (as he had the past three times) a legal precedent would have allowed any and all U.S. taxpayers to do what Starker had done. This has come to be known as a *reverse Starker exchange.*

If the IRS had wanted taxpayers to be able to do this they simply could have asked Congress to amend the tax law (Section 1031) to allow reverse exchanges. Starker's activities were published widely in the United States, and for the next 10–15 years the gurus of 1031 spent countless hours debating the merits and acceptable methods of conducting a reverse exchange; yet the deferred Starker exchange remained outside the laws, rules, and guidelines of Section 1031.

Over the years U.S. court cases from across the country had established that *like kind* meant that it was only possible to complete 1031 exchanges on residential property for residential property, commercial property for commercial property, vacant land for vacant land, a lot at the beach for a lot at the beach, and so on. This severely limited the ability to complete a tax-free exchange even within the concept of a deferred Starker exchange, because one had to buy replacement property whose use (zoning) was the same as the relinquished property sold.

In 1989 the congressional committee that oversaw the IRS requested that the IRS update and rewrite all 1031 exchange rules to make them more "user friendly," more fair, and in accordance with court decisions like *Starker.* The update was completed and the proposed rules, called the Deferred Exchange Regulations, were published on May 1, 1990, in the *Congressional Record.* These rules dramatically changed Section 1031. They established specific requirements to execute an exchange and redefined the meaning of "like kind" (as we shall discuss later). The publication of these rules was like opening the gate for a stampede of 1031 sales.

These proposed rules made mention of the reverse Starker exchange and promised guidelines would be published in the future.

In September 2000 (more than ten years later) the IRS published guidelines approving reverse Starker exchanges and outlined the rules under which a reverse exchange could be executed. These rules are very similar to the rules for a deferred exchange discussed in the next chapter.

While this course does not focus on reverse exchanges you should be aware that reverse exchanges are much more involved and require sophisticated tax advice. There are different types of reverse exchanges, such as build-to-suit exchanges, safe harbor reverse exchanges, and nonsafe harbor reverse exchanges.

case study

Lorenzo Duvalier is a real estate developer and investor whose principal residence is in Mesa, Arizona. He owns a second home in Denver and a strip mall in Boulder, Colorado, managed by his cousin. He has just completed construction of a small multiuse business/retail complex in Scottsdale, Arizona.

Lorenzo wants to sell some of his properties. In order to avoid large tax liabilities, he is considering the benefits of 1031 exchanges. Ari Hilliard, Lorenzo's broker, has just connected Lorenzo with Michelle Lanier, an investor who wants to exchange some of her investment properties in Phoenix. One in particular interests Lorenzo—a ten-year-old mansion worth $2.5 million, carrying a mortgage balance of $1.5 million.

Lorenzo instructs Ari to explore a 1031 exchange for the two properties.

1. Which of Lorenzo's properties would be eligible for a 1031 exchange?
   a. Principal residence in Mesa
   b. Strip mall in Boulder
   c. Multiuse complex in Scottsdale
   d. Second home in Denver

2. A 1031 exchange of properties between Lorenzo and Michelle would be calculated based on the
   a. mortgage balance.
   b. asking price.
   c. equity.
   d. appraised value.

Student Comments

Please provide your comments regarding the basic principle(s) addressed in this case study, and its relevance to the subject matter:

_____

_____

_____

■ Conclusion

The Starker activities revolutionized the 1031 world. From 1990 on, investors have taken increasing advantage of the new rules. More investors will follow as more real estate professionals, CPAs, attorneys, and investors become aware of the advantages of the 1031 rules. Simultaneous exchanges are still permitted but are rare. The deferred exchange is the most popular method today.

■ Chapter Three Review Questions

1. Which word is most closely associated with "Starker" in the 1031 exchange?
   - **a.** Deferred
   - **b.** Referred
   - **c.** Illegal
   - **d.** Simple

2. A taxpayer sells his second home (a lake cottage in northern Minnesota) to his lawyer. The taxpayer may avoid capital gains taxes by using Section 1031.
   - **a.** True
   - **b.** False

3. A builder, Bill Minton, bought 23 lots and built homes on each. All but one have sold to owner-occupants. Minton exchanges the last lot to Sonica Pewinski for her owner-occupied beach condo and certain other unspecified "boot." Will this transaction qualify under Section 1031?
   - **a.** Yes, because they are like-kind properties
   - **b.** No, because they are "inventory" properties
   - **c.** Yes, if all the timing requirements are satisfied
   - **d.** Yes, if Minton occupies his property for one year before the exchange

4. Generally, if a taxpayer wants to ensure that an exchange will be 100 percent tax free, the taxpayer must
   - **a.** buy up.
   - **b.** mortgage up.
   - **c.** spend all the money.
   - **d.** All of the above

5. "Boot" is taxable to the recipient in the year received.
   - **a.** True
   - **b.** False

6. The first acknowledged and recognized exchanges in the United States occurred in which decade?
   - **a.** 1880s
   - **b.** 1920s
   - **c.** 1950s
   - **d.** 1990s

7. Taxpayer Browder sells relinquished property with a loan balance of $125,000 and purchases replacement property with a new conventional loan of $80,000. With all other things being equal, taxpayer Browder will have how much "boot"?
   - **a.** There will be no "boot."
   - **b.** $45,000
   - **c.** $125,000
   - **d.** $80,000

8. A basic, simple, straight tax-free exchange is calculated based on the
   - **a.** sales/purchase price.
   - **b.** mortgage balance.
   - **c.** equity.
   - **d.** appraised value.

9. Another name for "boot" could be
   - **a.** unlike-kind property.
   - **b.** equity.
   - **c.** dealer.
   - **d.** qualified intermediary.

10. Kelley N. sells her investment property for $350,000. She has an existing mortgage of $87,000 and closing costs of $28,000. Which of the following purchases would result in no capital gains tax to Kelley?
    - **a.** Purchase of a $335,900 property using a new mortgage of $150,000
    - **b.** Purchase of a $400,000 property using a new mortgage of $85,000
    - **c.** Purchase of a $450,000 property using a new mortgage of $90,000
    - **d.** Purchase of a $380,000 property using a new mortgage of $160,000

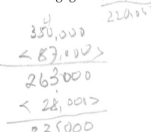

The Law and the Rules

overview

While the real estate agent is not the principal person responsible for the proper adherence to the tax law and the rules that govern Section 1031, familiarity with the rules will place the real estate agent in the position to "look over the shoulder" of the other parties (attorney, CPA, and client) to ensure that the client's activities result in a properly executed exchange. This chapter will focus further on the wording of Section 1031 of the Internal Revenue Code and the important rules pertaining to the law. ■

learning objectives

Upon completing this chapter you will be able to:

- describe the impact and meaning of the major words found in the law (e.g., *held, like-kind*);

- describe how leases for more than 30 years qualify for 1031 treatment;

- discuss the identification rule;

- discuss the three-property rule/200 percent rule/95 percent rule;

- discuss the 45-day clock;

- discuss the 180-day clock;

- describe the handling of the proceeds of sale and qualifications of the "safe harbor";

- explain the transfer of the cost basis and depreciation from the old to the new property; and

- briefly identify the rules for a personal property tax-free exchange.

■ Section 1031 of the Internal Revenue Code—The Law

As discussed in Chapter Three the actual wording in the IRS 1031 code is: "No gain or loss shall be recognized on the exchange of property *held* for productive use in a trade or business or for investment if such property is exchanged solely for property of a *like kind* which is to be *held* for productive use in a trade or business or for investment."

Before discussing the IRS rules let's review some of the key words to make sure we understand what they mean.

Held This word alone has caused thousand of court cases. Nowhere in the law does it specify exactly how long a taxpayer is supposed to have held (owned) the relinquished property before selling it as part of a 1031 exchange. Until a court case clarifies the issue it is wise to assume at least one full year of ownership. The law does say that in the case of a *"related exchange"*—where the taxpayer has exchanged with anyone related by blood or marriage or a partnership or corporation in which the taxpayer has a significant interest—the property must be "held" for two years. That means the taxpayer cannot even enter into a listing contract to sell the property during the two-year period.

After a tax-free exchange has been successfully completed how long must the taxpayer wait before disposing of (sell or exchange) the replacement property? There are as many answers to this as there are CPAs and attorneys. As a rule, use caution. If the taxpayer sells the replacement property within one year of the 1031 exchange, the taxpayer (if audited by the IRS) might be considered a dealer and the first tax-free exchange could be disallowed. This could be disastrous for the taxpayer. Always consult with a competent, experienced CPA or attorney before selling the recently acquired replacement property.

Like-Kind The most impressive result of the 1990 rewrite of Section 1031 has to do with the redefinition of *like-kind*. At that time the IRS decided that the rules resulting from the various court cases (residential for residential, commercial for commercial, and so on) were unnecessarily restrictive. The new rules allow a real estate tax-free exchange of *any real estate for any real estate* as long as it is "property used in the productive use in trade or business or investment property." The new rules do *not* allow an exchange of a principal residence, second home, time-share, or inventory property. This change had a tremendous impact on 1031. It is now legal to sell a residential investment and buy any other type of real estate (beach property, vacant land, commercial site, industrial property, mall, or strip center). The possibilities are endless.

Note: A common misconception is that accomplishing an exchange complicates a real estate closing. This is simply not true. Other than adding some wording to the sales contracts and a few extra papers to sign at closing (see Chapter Five), the sales should be as "normal" as any other real estate transaction.

The rewrite also said that *leases for more than 30 years qualified as real estate for 1031 tax-free exchange purposes.* This means that a 20-year lease with two 10-year options would qualify. Again, always consult a CPA on this.

If the taxpayer does what he or she thinks is an exchange, is audited by the IRS, and the IRS finds that the sales do *not* qualify for 1031 treatment because one or another of the rules was broken, the IRS will disallow the exchange. This means the IRS will not allow the deferral of tax liability afforded under Section 1031, and the taxpayer will have to pay the taxes, interest, and penalty. The taxpayer may not have the cash to pay these expenses because the taxpayer used all the proceeds to purchase additional property.

The 1031 rules have evolved, due to legislation and court decisions, to the point that with a little attention to detail any taxpayer can successfully complete a 1031 exchange, especially with the help of a 1031-experienced lawyer, a 1031-experienced CPA, a qualifying safe harbor (discussed later), and a knowledgeable real estate agent (you).

■ Section 1031—The Rules

Section 1031 outlines the rules to be followed if the real estate transactions are to qualify for deferral of gain.

45-Day Identification Rule

The day the relinquished (old) property closes an imaginary clock starts to tick. The replacement (new) property must be closed OR identified within 45 days of the closing of the relinquished property. This is the "45-day clock." The taxpayer must either close the purchase of the replacement property/properties within the 45 days or must *identify* the property or properties the taxpayer intends to purchase within the 45 days. The form used for identifying the property is included in Chapter Five.

In many deferred exchanges a taxpayer knows what property he or she wishes to purchase with the proceeds from the relinquished property. The purchase can be completed easily within the 45-day period, in which case no identification will be necessary. However, if the taxpayer is having a hard time locating suitable replacement properties, or he or she has found a suitable replacement property but cannot close the purchase within 45 days, the law allows the taxpayer to gain additional time by *"identifying"* the subject properties. In so doing the taxpayer is allowed a total of 180 days to complete the purchase. This is *not* an additional 180 days, but a total of 180 days (45 days plus 135 days).

Why would more time be needed? Why can't the purchase of the replacement property be accomplished within 45 days? As anyone in real estate knows, many real estate purchases can easily be closed in that time frame; however, should the taxpayer encounter legal problems, or problems in getting the deed signed, EPA issues, zoning changes, soil testing, survey issues, well water issues, percolation testing, building permits, or any number of other potential delays, he or she may find it impossible to close within 45 days. In this case the identification form (found in Chapter Five) is simply mailed or faxed to the "safe harbor" (discussed later in this chapter) within the 45 days.

If the taxpayer *identifies* certain properties and then discovers he or she cannot purchase them the taxpayer may change the property *identified* by using the same form and changing their selection of properties. Any changes to the *identified* property must be accomplished within the 45-day time period. After 45 days the taxpayer may not change the list of *identified* properties and must either purchase some or all (see the 95 percent rule in this chapter) of the properties on the identification form.

The *identification* must be reasonably specific, using a good legal description or a complete address, or describing the intended purchase with some degree of certainty. Do not, for example, *identify* by saying "48 acres south of Raleigh along U.S. Highway 64."

Note: It is recommended that taxpayers not *identify* until the 44th day in order to avoid having to repeatedly re-identify due to market conditions. If the purchase of the replacement property could be accomplished within the 45 days, the taxpayer would not *identify* at all.

Properties received during the "identification" period count toward the three-property, 200 percent, and 95 percent rule identification limits discussed in the next section. It is important to keep this in mind if you have already closed on one or two replacement properties and have run out of time. When you *identify* you may *identify* only one or two (depending on how many you have already closed on) additional properties.

Three-Property, 200 Percent, and 95 Percent Rules

These rules only apply when a taxpayer *identifies* replacement properties. If the taxpayer is able to purchase all replacement properties within the 45-day clock time period, these rules do not apply. (The rules are difficult rules to understand, as they actually make 1031 more complicated, when it seemed that Congress and the IRS wanted to simplify 1031.)

Some taxpayers will sell one relinquished property and purchase one replacement property. Easy! What if a taxpayer has multiple properties to sell? The taxpayer may sell these relinquished properties in separate transactions, doing a tax-free exchange for each relinquished property. The taxpayer may also sell multiple properties and combine them into one tax-free exchange. Timing is critical on this.

Some taxpayers will sell multiple relinquished properties all as part of the same 1031 exchange. The taxpayer may purchase any number and any total value of replacement properties as long as the purchases close within the 45 days after the sale of the first relinquished properties.

If you need additional time to close the purchase of the replacement properties and obtain the time by "identifying," the following rules apply. Regardless of the number of relinquished properties involved, the taxpayer must meet one of the three alternative rules.

Alternative 1: Three-Property Rule   If you *identify* no more than three properties, the replacement properties may be of any value, individually or collectively. It is important to keep this in mind if the taxpayer has already closed on one or two replacement properties but runs out of time. Properties acquired during the 45-day period count towards the three-property rule and limit how many properties should be *identified.*

Alternative 2: 200 Percent Rule   If the taxpayer identifies more properties than allowed by the three-property rule, the total value of all purchased replacement properties may not exceed 200 percent of the total sales price of all relinquished properties. Properties acquired during the 45-day period count toward the 200 percent rule requirement and limit the value of properties *identified.* (The taxpayer needs a contract or appraisal to prove this if audited.)

Alternative 3: 95 Percent Rule   If the taxpayer *identifies* more properties than allowed by the three-property rule, and the 200 percent rule has been exceeded, the taxpayer must purchase, by the end of the exchange period, enough replacement properties to equal at least 95 percent of the fair market value of the identified replacement properties. This limits the taxpayer's ability to identify a large list of potential replacement properties and close on those most convenient. Properties acquired during the identification period (45 days) count toward the 95 percent rule and limit the number of properties that should be *identified.*

Summary of Alternatives   If you *identify,* your transaction must comply with one of the three alternatives described. In real life, the taxpayer, real estate agent, attorney, or CPA must be aware of this rule and make sure things are done correctly at this stage. Planning is crucial to the successful execution of a 1031 tax-free exchange.

It is in the regulations that during the first 45 days and without the identification form being used by the taxpayer, the taxpayer can purchase an unlimited amount of properties of any purchase price. In other words the rules discussed (three-property rule, 200 percent rule, and 95 percent rule) do not apply.

So, if taxpayer Jones sold one replacement property for $1,000,000 on January 1, 2008, he could buy 37 lots for $3,000,000 if the purchases closed by February 14, 2008. Taxpayer Jones has exceeded the three-property rule, the 200 percent rule, and the 95 percent rule but they do not apply since the taxpayer did not identify and closed all purchases within the first 45 days.

Conversely, if taxpayer Jones identified the 37 lots where the seller was asking $3,100,000 and ended up purchasing 36 lots for $2,900,000 before the 180th day, Jones would have

- *broken the three-property rule (he sold only one, for $1,000,000),*
- *broken the 200 percent rule (200% of $1,000,000 = $2,000,000), and*
- *qualified the purchase under the 95 percent rule ($2,950,000 ÷ $3,100,000 = 95.16%).*

180-Day Rule

Once the taxpayer *identifies,* additional time is provided to close the purchases of the replacement property. The rule is a little more involved than it appears. For any sale of relinquished properties in the first months of the year (January 1–June 30) the 180-day rule is simple. For closings that occur after July 1—particularly those in late October, November, or December—the prudent agent should be particularly careful. The 180-day rule states that if you can identify, you are allowed 180 days to close the replacement property *OR* up to the date that year's income tax return is due (April 15 for individuals but varying dates for many partnerships, corporations, etc.). Thus an individual selling a relinquished property on December 28 does not have 180 days to complete the exchange. That person has until April 15 of the next year, or about 109 days. What if the taxpayer could not get the purchase closed by day 109 (April 15)? It is possible to request an extension for the 1040 income tax return, giving the taxpayer an additional 71 days to close the purchase of the replacement property.

No extensions are allowed under the 180-day rule. If the 180th day falls on a Saturday, Sunday, or legal holiday, or your attorney was sick, you should have closed the purchase of the replacement property on the previous Friday. Under all circumstances the agent, taxpayer, CPA, and attorneys must be aware of these rules and take whatever actions necessary to close the purchase of the replacement property or properties.

Note: When a property is being "taken" by a government authority (highway commission, school board, and so forth) the law often gives the taxpayer two years to reinvest without having to pay capital gains taxes. See your CPA if you think you qualify for the longer time period.

Proceeds of Sale of the Relinquished Property

Any money resulting from the sale of the relinquished property not invested in the replacement property will go to the taxpayer. It is called *boot* and it is taxable to the recipients (taxpayer) in the year *received*. Earlier it was suggested that the taxpayer "spend *all* the money." Any money received by the taxpayer is taxable but will be partially offset by deductible closing expenses. If a taxpayer wants to execute a 1031 exchange he or she must not touch the money. This holds true for the 180-day period, even if a taxpayer has purchased the desired replacement properties and wants the remaining money sent to him or her. Remember that if the taxpayer does not create a mortgage on the replacement property larger than paid off on the sale of the relinquished property the difference in the mortgage amounts is boot also. In order to purchase a more expensive replacement property the taxpayer may use a mortgage or personal funds to close the purchase.

Safe Harbor/Qualified Intermediary

What is the status of the proceeds of sale after closing on the relinquished property, and before closing on the replacement property? One hard and fast rule is that the *taxpayer may not be in either actual or constructive receipt of the money.*

The regulations say that the proceeds must be with a "qualified intermediary" or "safe harbor." Prior to the closing of the relinquished property (definitely before the deed is recorded) the taxpayer must enter into an "exchange agreement" with a qualified intermediary/safe harbor or the IRS may say the taxpayer was in "constructive" receipt of the proceeds of sale and disallow the tax-free exchange.

Should the IRS audit a taxpayer following completion of a 1031 (just because a taxpayer executed a 1031 does NOT mean the taxpayer is more likely to be audited), the auditor will first check is to see who the safe harbor was. If the safe harbor does not qualify, the 1031 is disallowed—and serious tax problems for the taxpayer result as the capital gain tax is now due, with additional penalties and interest. The safe harbor rule is very important.

There are four safe harbors:

1. Security or guarantee arrangements
2. Qualified escrow accounts and qualified trusts
3. Qualified intermediaries
4. Interest and growth factors

The use of qualified intermediaries (safe harbor #3) is by far the most common. For the sake of simplicity the term *safe harbor* is used throughout this text. That term refers to a qualified intermediary type of safe harbor.

Who Qualifies as a Safe Harbor? The list of qualifiers is long and includes the following:

- Any CPA in the country, as long as the CPA has not performed any work for the taxpayer for the past two years
- Any attorney in the country, as long as the attorney has not performed any work for the taxpayer for the past two years
- Any trust department of any bank, as long as it has not been the bank of the taxpayer for the past two years
- Companies established to act as safe harbors, such as Investors Title Exchange Corporation, Lawyers Title Exchange, and Starker Exchanges

The function of the safe harbor is to "dock" the proceeds of sale in a reliable account; pay interest on the funds if agreed upon in the "exchange agreement" (see the example in Chapter Five); disburse these funds to close the purchase of replacement properties at the direction of the taxpayer or the taxpayer's representative (attorney or CPA); and account to the taxpayer for the funds.

Many firms and individuals may act as qualified intermediaries/safe harbors. As mentioned above, in the event a taxpayer is audited by the IRS, one of the first things the IRS agent investigates is the choice of a safe harbor. If the choice does not qualify as a safe harbor nothing else matters. The exchange is disallowed and taxes, interest, and penalty are due. Many times closing attorneys have been used as the safe harbor. This is not a good idea even if the attorney offers services free of charge—authorities are currently looking for an attorney from Florida who stole $6.2 million from a 1031 client, and another from California who took more than $30 million.

Although the vast majority of attorneys are honest, professional safe harbors are recommended because they have the necessary forms, will place the money in an interest-bearing account, and will have the money available for the closing. Any private attorney or CPA employed as a safe harbor should be bonded, and most agents and taxpayers are uncomfortable demanding or requesting this safeguard.

One of the 1031 rules states that the safe harbor will "step into the shoes" of the seller/client/taxpayer. This is merely a technicality. For the safe harbor to step into the shoes, the contract on the sale of the relinquished property, as well as the contract for the purchase of the replacement property, *must* allow for the assignment of the client's rights as seller of the relinquished property and buyer of the replacement property. Suggested wording for the sales contract can be found in Chapter Five. The seller/client/taxpayer of the relinquished property does not deed the property to the safe harbor; he or she deeds it directly to the buyer. The seller of the replacement property does not deed the property to the safe harbor; he or she deeds it directly to the buyer/client/taxpayer. In other types of 1031 exchanges the safe harbor does take title.

The safe harbor/qualified intermediary generally does not give tax advice. He or she does not communicate with the taxpayer directly but works through a CPA, personal attorney, or closing attorney. Safe harbors are employed to perform a limited function (to hold the proceeds of sale and disburse them as instructed). The taxpayer may use the same safe harbor two or more times in the same year.

■ Additional 1031 Rules

Interest-Bearing Account

The law allows the safe harbor to place the money in an interest-bearing account. The interest goes to the taxpayer when the account is closed. The taxpayer receives a 1099 statement and must pay taxes on the interest income. This issue should be addressed in the contract between the safe harbor and the taxpayer (Exchange Agreement; see forms in Chapter Five).

Cost Basis

The cost basis of the relinquished property is carried over to the replacement property. If multiple properties are involved the cost basis is distributed on a pro rata basis. The taxpayer's CPA does the computing.

Depreciation

In spite of what many of us have been told, the taxpayer does not "start over" with the depreciation schedule on the replacement property. The taxpayer's CPA will *recompute* the allowable depreciation based upon the present tax laws on depreciation schedules. This could provide additional depreciation and a tax shelter for the taxpayer depending on the particular circumstances.

The advice to "buy up, mortgage up, and spend all the money," if taken, may produce more tax shelter/depreciation for the taxpayer. In addition, a taxpayer may elect to continue to use his or her existing depreciation schedule from the relinquished property as the depreciation for the replacement property. Any additional basis must be depreciated using the MACRS (Modified Accelerated Continued Recovering System) rules (27.5-year residential; 39-year commercial).

Note: If the taxpayer has depreciation remaining from the relinquished property and purchases vacant land, he or she carries over the remaining depreciation to the replacement (vacant land) property. Thus the taxpayer is depreciating property on an exchange that the taxpayer would not have been able to depreciate had the taxpayer purchased the vacant land property on a normal purchase. Again, talk to your tax professional about this issue before acting on it.

Issues Relating to 1031 Eligibility

One controversial subject is that of timber. Despite the fact that many state laws define uncut timber as real estate and the fact that exchange of uncut timber for a fee simple interest in other investment real estate seems to qualify for 1031 treatment, the IRS and some court decisions disagree. May a taxpayer execute a personal property tax-free exchange for cut or uncut timber in exchange for lumber to be delivered to the same real estate in order to build a building? This question remains unanswered. If your clients ask you about this refer them to a qualified tax expert.

To qualify for 1031 tax-free exchange treatment the relinquished property and the replacement property must be in the United States, Washington, DC, or U.S. territories (domestic exchange). Property not in the United States, Washington, DC, or U.S. territories can qualify for a foreign exchange. Domestic exchange property is not "like-kind" to foreign exchange property.

South Carolina has repealed a long-standing law that prohibited a taxpayer from using the tax-free exchange law to avoid South Carolina capital gains taxes if the replacement property was not in South Carolina. This *state* prohibition could exist even though the sale qualified for 1031 *federal* tax treatment. Georgia, Mississippi, and Vermont bar exchanges if out-of-state property is involved, and Indiana bars deferred exchanges if an intermediary is involved. Other states may have their own rules. Always check with a CPA on state laws that might prohibit exchanging out-of-state properties.

It is permissible to purchase a lot and hire a builder to construct improvements. If the improvements cannot be completed by the 180th day, *close the purchase!* The IRS will count only the cost of the lot and the finished improvements as of the day of closing for the 1031 purpose. Make sure when you *identify* that you be specific about what is to be built—4-bedroom, 3-bath, 2,679-square-foot, 2-story home, for example. Make sure the contract with the builder says something about a tax-free exchange and a penalty clause for not completing the improvements in a timely manner. Under any circumstances close the transaction before the 180th day.

Title Rule

Whoever has title to the relinquished property must take title to the replacement property. Although there are exceptions to this rule, you should be careful if your attorney says you may deed out of a partnership or corporation into individuals shortly before conveying to the buyer. You may have violated the "held" rule; that is, the new owner entity did not hold title for a sufficiently long period of time to meet 1031 requirements even though the partnership or corporation owned the property for many years.

A husband who owned property prior to marriage should take title to replacement property in his name only (consider single member LLC), not in the name of husband and wife, even if the wife signed the deed to the relinquished property. Two brothers who owned property together might have a "partnership" even though they do not consider it a partnership, so they must buy replacement property *together*. It is not permissible for one brother to do a tax-free exchange and the other brother to pay capital gains tax.

Reducing Future Tax Liability

A client may ask if there is a way to reduce permanently or almost eliminate the tax liability on the future sale of a property. The following example provides an answer.

> *A taxpayer wishes to sell a 16-unit apartment complex (investment property) but faces a huge capital gains tax liability. The taxpayer decides to complete a tax-free exchange by purchasing five single-family investment properties (replacement properties). These single-family properties are currently rented to tenants. After waiting at least three years the taxpayer may move into one of these properties, occupy it for two years as a principal residence, sell it, and take the $250,000/$500,000 exclusion allowed on the sale of a principal residence. The taxpayer may then move into another of the five homes, use it for two years as the principal residence, sell it, and take an additional $250,000/$500,000 exclusion. The taxpayer may continue in this manner until all five homes are sold. Note that the taxpayer would not eliminate all tax liability; there would be a tax of 25 percent (recapture) on the depreciation taken after May 7, 1997. Nevertheless, the potential is there for the taxpayer to reduce the overall tax liability significantly.*

In the above example, the taxpayer sold the 16-unit apartment complex and successfully completed a 1031 tax-free exchange. Then after waiting three years he or she moved into one of the single-family homes and made it his or her principal residence, hoping to qualify for Section 121's $250,000/500,000 exclusion. On October 22, 2004, Congress clarified this point and said that when a taxpayer wants to combine the use of 1031 and Section 121 the taxpayer must own the replacement property for *five* years and occupy it for *two* years to qualify for the $250,000/500,000 exclusion. Thus it is important that the taxpayer knows this and complies with it even against the advice of experts to the contrary.

Replacement Property Issues

While it is clear that a taxpayer *may not* sell relinquished property and use the proceeds to make improvements to property the taxpayer already owns (1031 anticipates the purchase of new property in the exchange), what is not so clear are the rules about using funds from the sale of a relinquished property to improve replacement property that needs work or that is vacant. If the contract for sale on the replacement property calls for the seller to rehabilitate the structure as part of the purchase price (using bids from contractors selected by the taxpayer) and the purchase price reflects these costs, the taxpayer is in a good position. If the taxpayer wants to supervise or complete the repairs after taking title, the repairs must be accomplished and the money disbursed within the 180-day time period. Questions arise as to the mechanics of the repairs. Should the taxpayer close the purchase and place the funds from the safe harbor in the closing attorney's escrow/trust account to be disbursed when the repairs are completed, and, if so, would this satisfy the 1031 requirements? May the taxpayer leave the "repair funds" in the safe harbor until the repairs are completed, knowing that the funds must be disbursed before the 180th day? Answers to these questions should be requested from the taxpayer's CPA.

A question frequently asked by students concerning tax-free exchanges is, "Can I execute a tax-free exchange to purchase my retirement home at the beach (in the mountains or a golf community)?" The answer is, "Talk to your CPA." After that I remind the student that a principal residence, second home, and inventory property CANNOT qualify for a tax-free exchange either as the relinquished or the replacement property. Having said that, I propose the student, after consulting with his or her tax advisor, consider the following route:

1. Sell the relinquished property and put the proceeds of sale in a qualified intermediary/safe harbor.
2. Proceed to find a property for sale that would make a wonderful retirement home.
3. Purchase it as a replacement property for the tax-free exchange using some or all of the money resulting from the sale of the relinquished property, remembering to create mortgages equal to or greater than the mortgages paid off in the sale of the relinquished property.
4. Rent the property out as "property held for the productive use in trade or business" (what most of us call investment property).

It is advised to keep it as a rental for at least three years, and if the student still desires to do so, move into the property as his or her retirement home. If he or she lives there for at least two years he or she would qualify for the Section 121 exclusion of $250,000/500,000 upon the sale of that property.

Personal Property Tax-Free Exchange

All personal property has been placed in 15 classes just as real estate has been placed in 4 classes as discussed earlier. The taxpayer may only exchange *within* the same class of property. The taxpayer may exchange a car for a car or a truck for a truck, but the taxpayer may not exchange a car for a truck. A taxpayer may exchange a computer for a computer or a copying machine for a copying machine; but the taxpayer may not exchange a computer for a copying machine. A thoroughbred horse may be exchanged for an old gray mare only if they are the same gender; animals of different genders are not "like kind."

The following is a story concerning the completion of a 1031 exchange. In this case personal property made a difference in the IRS's treatment of the transaction. Corporation A wanted to sell its corporate building to a purchaser for $1,000,000. The sale produced the following paperwork: the sales contract, the appraisal, and the HUD-1 closing statement. After selling the building (relinquished property) the proceeds were placed with a safe harbor, and Corporation A entered into a contract to purchase Corporation B's building for $1,200,000 (replacement property). While this appears to be a good tax-free exchange, when Corporation A's income *tax return was audited by the IRS, a portion of the tax-free exchange was not allowed. Corporation A had to pay taxes, interest, and penalties with respect to the sale of $200,000 worth of personal property (boot). What personal property? The appraisal stated that the $1,000,000 value comprised $800,000 real estate and $200,000 personal property, listed as telephone systems, computer systems, copiers, and an old truck. The sad part of this story is that after purchasing the new building, Corporation A had to spend about $250,000 on a new telephone system, computer system, copiers, and a truck.*

A real estate agent knowledgeable about 1031 exchanges and involved with this sale could have acted in the following manner. The agent would make an offer to Corporation B to purchase the building for $1,450,000, on condition that at closing the building would have a newly installed telephone system, computer system, copiers, and a truck. Estimates for each of these items would be attached to the offer. The contract would have a $250,000 nonrefundable earnest money deposit (good-faith money, hand money). The deposit would be forfeited in the event Corporation A did not close. Corporation B would jump at the opportunity to sell under these conditions. Corporation A would accomplish a real estate 1031 exchange ($800,000 for $1,200,000) and four personal property exchanges ($200,000 for $250,000). Corporation A would avoid any boot and thus would avoid taxes, interest, and penalties on $200,000. The agent would certainly have earned the commission on this transaction.

case study A

Ron Perillo runs a fishing operation in Key West, Florida. He is thrilled one day when he learns that his biggest competitor, Butch Ordoñez, is shutting down his fishing operation and moving to Orlando. Ron has had his eye on some of Butch's new rigs and wants to purchase them as soon as Butch makes them available. Ron owns a few small residential investment properties in Miami that he plans to sell to finance the purchases. Ron asks his broker, Tina Baker, to refresh his memory about the requirements of Section 1031.

Tina explains to Ron that Section 1031 of the Internal Revenue Code says that gain or loss is not recognized when property held for investment or for productive use in trade or business is exchanged solely for property of a like kind to be held either for investment or for productive use in trade or business. Ron is convinced he can meet the requirements of 1031 and tells Tina to move forward with the transaction. Tina thinks there might be a problem.

1. Tina probably is concerned that the exchange does not meet the "like kind" standard because
   a. a fishing rig is not "like kind" to real estate.
   b. commercial property is not eligible under Section 1031.
   c. it is illegal to sell multiple residential properties and then purchase only one replacement property.
   d. investment property may not be exchanged for commercial property.

2. Butch Ordoñez also owns the building from which he runs his fishing operations. This includes some docking facilities. If Ron wishes to execute a 100 percent tax-free transaction, he must

   a. either purchase or identify the property within 180 days.

   b. identify additional properties other than those owned by Butch.

   c. buy up, mortgage up, and spend all the money.

   d. use the attorney who will close the real estate transaction as his qualified intermediary.

Student Comments

Please provide your comments regarding the basic principle(s) addressed in this case study, and its relevance to the subject matter:

_____

_____

_____

case study B

Benjamin Beckman is in the process of conducting a 1031 exchange for his tool shop in Norman, Oklahoma. He plans to relinquish the shop to ToolWorks Amalgamated, located about a mile away from his shop. In exchange, Amalgamated plans to replace the shop with the wholesale hardware store it opened next door to Benjamin last year.

Benjamin has told his broker, Walt Corigliano, not to worry about Section 1031's "safe harbor" requirements because he has everything under control. Benjamin plans to "dock" the proceeds of the sale of his tool shop in a reliable account, take care of any interest on the funds if necessary, disburse the funds when it's time to close on the purchase of ToolWorks, and account to the IRS for the funds.

Walt gently tells Benjamin that he is missing the point of the "safe harbor" rules.

1. The primary reason a seller needs a "safe harbor" to hold the proceeds of a 1031 exchange is that

   a. the IRS must approve the 1031 exchange before the parties may complete it.

   b. any taxes owed will be handled through the "safe harbor."

   c. unethical and illegal activity is common in 1031 exchanges.

   d. the taxpayer may not be in either actual or constructive receipt of the money.

2. The most common type of "safe harbor" is

   a. qualified intermediary.

   b. security or guarantee arrangements.

   c. qualified escrow account and qualified trust.

   d. interest and growth factor.

Student Comments

Please provide your comments regarding the basic principle(s) addressed in this case study, and its relevance to the subject matter:

_____

_____

_____

■ Conclusion

By now you can appreciate the huge impact the Section 1031 tax-free exchange has had and will continue to have on the sale of real estate. As more agents and investors learn of these laws and rules, more will take advantage of them. These laws and rules may seem involved at first but they can be mastered to the extent that you will be able to discuss them with your clients and refer your clients to competent and experienced professionals.

■ Chapter Four Review Questions

1. All tax-free exchanges are required to be finalized within how many days from the closing of the "old" property?

   a. 90

   b. 180

   c. 225

   d. 365

2. It is a requirement of Section 1031 that the "safe harbor" receive an assignment of the taxpayer's rights in all sales contracts on the subject properties.

   a. True

   b. False

3. David Jones exchanged his investment condo in New York for Jay Anderson's NASCAR racing car. The IRS will probably

   a. approve this exchange.

   b. disallow this exchange because both properties are not in the same state.

   c. approve this exchange as long as no boot was involved.

   d. disallow this exchange because they are not like-kind properties.

4. The sale of taxpayer Jones's apartment building in Philadelphia closes on June 1, 2008. If Jones wants to *identify*, when must the *identification* be finalized?

   a. 7 days

   b. 14 days

   c. 30 days

   d. 45 days

5. Both the replacement and relinquished properties involved in a Section 1031 exchange must be in the United States, Washington, DC, and the U.S. Territories.

   a. True

   b. False

6. With respect to a *personal property* tax-free exchange a taxpayer would be allowed to exchange his 1996 business truck for a 1998 model copying machine.

   a. True

   b. False

7. The money or proceeds of the sale of the "old" property may be deposited in the taxpayer's bank account until "new" properties are acquired.

   a. True

   b. False

8. Leases qualify for 1031 treatment if the duration is more than

   a. 10 years.

   b. 30 years.

   c. 1 year.

   d. 99 years.

9. The 1031 law says that if you *identify* and buy more than three properties, the total purchase price of the replacement properties must not exceed

   a. 50 percent of the relinquished property sales price.

   b. 100 percent of the relinquished property sales price.

   c. 150 percent of the relinquished property sales price.

   d. 200 percent of the relinquished property sales price.

10. The 1031 law says that if you *do NOT identify* but you close the purchase of the replacement property within 45 days of the closing of the sale of the relinquished property, you can purchase which of the following?

    a. An unlimited dollar amount of real estate

    b. No more than the amount of the relinquished property

    c. No more than 200 percent of the amount of the relinquished property

    d. No more than 400 percent of the amount of the relinquished property

The Paperwork

This chapter introduces key forms used when executing a 1031 exchange. The goal is to familiarize you with the forms and show when they affect the real estate sales transaction. All forms discussed in this section are located at the end of this chapter. You may wish to review the forms and then read the following discussion for a clearer understanding of each form's purpose. ■

learning objectives

Upon completing this chapter you will be able to:

- describe the IRS Form 8824 Tax-Free Exchange;

- describe the wording needed in the various contracts of sale for the relinquished and replacement property;

- explain the purpose of the exchange agreement; and

- describe the use of the property assignment forms and the addendum to closing statement form.

■ IRS Form 8824: Like-Kind Exchange

This is a form the taxpayer must submit with his or her 1040 income tax return showing that a like-kind exchange has been executed. Note that the form is letter size and one page (front and back). The CPA/tax professional fills it out from information provided by the taxpayer, but it is not overly involved and should not add much to the fees charged by the CPA/tax professional. A copy is included in Figure 5.1 on pages 47–51.

■ Suggested Language for Standard Real Estate Contracts

■ When listing the relinquished property it is a good idea, although not required, to include wording in the listing contract that the seller intends to execute a 1031 tax-free exchange in connection with the sale of this property. This shows the seller's intention at the time of listing. For example: *"It is the intention of the Seller to qualify this sale under section 1031 of the Internal Revenue Code."*

■ When a buyer is found for the relinquished property, some wording must be inserted into the sales contract showing that the seller intends to execute an exchange and that the buyer agrees that the seller may assign the seller's rights to his or her safe harbor/qualified intermediary. For example: *"The Seller desires to effect a like-kind exchange for the property transferred under this contract; and the Buyer and Seller agree that, notwithstanding any provision to the contrary, the Seller's rights, title, and interests under this contract may be assigned to (here you name the safe harbor if known at this time or put in "a safe harbor to be designated in the future")."*

■ When you find a replacement property for the taxpayer/client, wording must be inserted in the offer for the replacement property to show that the buyer intends to execute an exchange and that the seller agrees that the buyer may assign the buyer's right to his or her safe harbor. For example: *"The Buyer desires to effect a like-kind exchange involving the real property to be transferred to Buyer pursuant to this contract; and the Buyer and Seller agree that, notwithstanding any provision to the contrary, Buyer's rights, title, and interests under this contract may be assigned to (here you name the safe harbor)."*

Note: While clients may not know which safe harbor they intend to use when they list the property, or when they enter into a contract of sale of the relinquished property, they should know who they are going to use by the time they enter into a contract to purchase the replacement property or they probably have not executed the exchange correctly.

Note: Some contract forms already have language similar to the above. In that case, additional wording is not needed.

■ The Exchange Agreement

The exchange agreement below must be entered into before the closing of the relinquished property. This is a contract between a taxpayer/client and the safe harbor wherein the parties agree to a number of things, including

1. that the safe harbor will act as the safe harbor;
2. the fee to be charged;
3. that the taxpayer/client is executing a 1031 exchange;
4. that the funds will or will not be placed in an interest-bearing account, and whether the taxpayer or the safe harbor is to receive the interest;
5. when the taxpayer/client can demand the funds;
6. the termination date of the exchange agreement;
7. liability issues;
8. normal legal paragraphs; and
9. the signature page.

A sample exchange agreement appears in Figure 5.2 on pages 52–58.

Note: The taxpayer needs to find a "safe harbor/qualified intermediary" and enter into the exchange agreement around the time the contract for the sale of the relinquished property is signed. The taxpayer may look for an acceptable safe harbor prior to this time but most safe harbors do not want to enter into the exchange agreement until a buyer is found.

The taxpayer must be diligent in finding a safe harbor because once the sale of the relinquished property is closed it is too late (taxpayer is in receipt of the proceeds of sale). Also, steps that should have been taken or documents that should have been signed at closing may not have been accomplished properly due to a lack of knowledge by the taxpayer and his or her agent. Having a safe harbor to guide the taxpayer is critically important at this point.

■ Exhibits to the Exchange Agreement

There are three exhibits to the exchange agreement:

- ■ Exhibit A: Relinquished Property Description of *all* property to be sold as part of the 1031 exchange (Figure 5.3 on page 59)
- ■ Exhibit B: IRS Form W-9 showing the taxpayer/client Social Security number or tax ID number (Figure 5.4 on pages 60–63)
- ■ Exhibit C: Replacement Property Identification Form to be used if additional time (180-day rule) is desired to close the purchase of replacement properties. This form may never actually be utilized (Figure 5.5 on page 64).

■ Relinquished Property Assignment

This is to be signed by the taxpayer/client (seller), a representative of the safe harbor, and the buyer of the relinquished property. The safe harbor steps into the shoes of the taxpayer/client. The safe harbor receives the proceeds of sale. Note that the taxpayer/client seller deeds the property directly to the purchaser and the safe harbor never takes title to the property in this type of 1031 exchange. Figure 5.6 on page 65 contains the Relinquished Property Assignment.

■ Replacement Property Assignment

This is to be signed by the taxpayer/client (buyer), a representative of the safe harbor, and the seller of the replacement property. As noted, the safe harbor steps into the shoes of the taxpayer/client and the safe harbor technically becomes the buyer. The safe harbor produces the funds necessary to purchase the property. Note that the seller deeds the property directly to the taxpayer/client. The safe harbor never takes title to the property in this type of 1031 exchange. Any mortgages needed to close the purchase of the replacement property are the obligation of the taxpayer/client. A Replacement Property Assignment form is shown in Figure 5.7 on page 66.

■ Addendum to Closing Statement

The safe harbor sends this form to the closing attorney. It is to be signed by the taxpayer/client (purchaser), the safe harbor representative, and the seller of the replacement property. The form, Figure 5.8 on page 67, says that the safe harbor is involved in the transaction for 1031 purposes only.

◼ Computing Capital Gain and Tax Due (Form)

This form, Figure 5.9 on page 68, is also located in Chapter One to assist the agent in computing the approximate capital gain on the sale of real estate. The information to compute the capital gain is provided by the taxpayer and is probably not accurate. That is acceptable in that the agent is only trying to approximate the capital gain and is *not* attempting to file a tax return.

◼ Conclusion

The scope of this subject is much greater than this basic overview could possibly explore. Education can be defined as "knowing when to seek help from an expert." In the final analysis properly executed tax-free exchanges under Section 1031 are a fantastic method for the deferment of taxes, creation of additional tax shelters, maintaining net worth, and reorganization of assets. After mastering the main concepts of this text and retaining it for reference in the future, you will be ready to discuss this wonderful subject with your clients.

■ Chapter Five Review Questions

1. The "exchange agreement" is signed by
   a. the buyer and seller.
   b. the buyer, the seller, and the safe harbor.
   c. the seller and the safe harbor.
   d. None of the above

2. It is a requirement of Section 1031 of the Internal Revenue Code that the "safe harbor" be assigned the rights of the taxpayer in the sale of the relinquished property and the purchase of the replacement property.
   a. True
   b. False

3. In what document would the parties agree to permit the assignment of the rights of a party to another person or entity?
   a. The deed
   b. The exchange agreement
   c. The closing documents
   d. The sales contract

4. Which is NOT addressed in the "exchange agreement"?
   a. The fees the safe harbor will charge
   b. The fact that the safe harbor will have liability for property conditions
   c. Interest earned on the money
   d. The "identification" procedures

5. Which is NOT an addendum to the "exchange agreement"?
   a. The replacement property "identification" forms
   b. A copy of the sales contract
   c. IRS W-2 form showing the taxpayer's Social Security number or tax ID number
   d. A description of all relinquished property

Figure 5.1 | Form 8824: Like-Kind Exchanges

Form **8824**	**Like-Kind Exchanges**	OMB No. 1545-1190
Department of the Treasury Internal Revenue Service	**(and section 1043 conflict-of-interest sales)** ▶ **Attach to your tax return.**	20**06** Attachment Sequence No. **109**

Name(s) shown on tax return	Identifying number

Part I   Information on the Like-Kind Exchange

Note: *If the property described on line 1 or line 2 is real or personal property located outside the United States, indicate the country.*

1 Description of like-kind property given up ▶ ....

2 Description of like-kind property received ▶ ....

3 Date like-kind property given up was originally acquired (month, day, year) . . . . . . **3** / /

4 Date you actually transferred your property to other party (month, day, year) . . . . . . **4** / /

5 Date like-kind property you received was identified by written notice to another party (month, day, year). See instructions for 45-day written notice requirement . . . . . . **5** / /

6 Date you actually received the like-kind property from other party (month, day, year). See instructions **6** / /

7 Was the exchange of the property given up or received made with a related party, either directly or indirectly (such as through an intermediary)? See instructions. If "Yes," complete Part II. If "No," go to Part III . . . ☐ **Yes** ☐ **No**

Part II   **Related Party Exchange Information**

8 Name of related party	Relationship to you	Related party's identifying number
Address (no., street, and apt., room, or suite no., city or town, state, and ZIP code)		

9 During this tax year (and before the date that is 2 years after the last transfer of property that was part of the exchange), did the related party directly or indirectly (such as through an intermediary) sell or dispose of any part of the like-kind property received from you in the exchange? . . . . ☐ **Yes** ☐ **No**

10 During this tax year (and before the date that is 2 years after the last transfer of property that was part of the exchange), did you sell or dispose of any part of the like-kind property you received? . . . . ☐ **Yes** ☐ **No**

*If both lines 9 and 10 are "No" and this is the year of the exchange, go to Part III. If both lines 9 and 10 are "No" and this is **not** the year of the exchange, stop here. If either line 9 or line 10 is "Yes," complete Part III and report on this year's tax return the deferred gain or (loss) from line 24 **unless** one of the exceptions on line 11 applies.*

11 If one of the exceptions below applies to the disposition, check the applicable box:

a ☐ The disposition was after the death of either of the related parties.

b ☐ The disposition was an involuntary conversion, and the threat of conversion occurred after the exchange.

c ☐ You can establish to the satisfaction of the IRS that neither the exchange nor the disposition had tax avoidance as its principal purpose. If this box is checked, attach an explanation (see instructions).

For Paperwork Reduction Act Notice, see page 5. | Cat. No. 12311A | Form **8824** (2006)

Figure 5.1 | Form 8824: Like-Kind Exchanges (continued)

Form 8824 (2006)   Page **2**

Name(s) shown on tax return. Do not enter name and social security number if shown on other side. | Your social security number

Part III   **Realized Gain or (Loss), Recognized Gain, and Basis of Like-Kind Property Received**

Caution: *If you transferred and received (a) more than one group of like-kind properties or (b) cash or other (not like-kind) property, see **Reporting of multi-asset exchanges** in the instructions.*

Note: *Complete lines 12 through 14 **only** if you gave up property that was not like-kind. Otherwise, go to line 15.*

12   Fair market value (FMV) of other property given up **12**

13   Adjusted basis of other property given up **13**

14   Gain or (loss) recognized on other property given up. Subtract line 13 from line 12. Report the gain or (loss) in the same manner as if the exchange had been a sale **14**

     Caution: *If the property given up was used previously or partly as a home, see **Property used as home** in the instructions.*

15   Cash received, FMV of other property received, plus net liabilities assumed by other party, reduced (but not below zero) by any exchange expenses you incurred (see instructions) **15**

16   FMV of like-kind property you received **16**

17   Add lines 15 and 16 . . . .   **17**

18   Adjusted basis of like-kind property you gave up, net amounts paid to other party, plus any exchange expenses **not** used on line 15 (see instructions) **18**

19   **Realized gain or (loss).** Subtract line 18 from line 17 . . . .   **19**

20   Enter the smaller of line 15 or line 19, but not less than zero **20**

21   Ordinary income under recapture rules. Enter here and on Form 4797, line 16 (see instructions) .   **21**

22   Subtract line 21 from line 20. If zero or less, enter -0-. If more than zero, enter here and on Schedule D or Form 4797, unless the installment method applies (see instructions) **22**

23   **Recognized gain.** Add lines 21 and 22 . . . .   **23**

24   Deferred gain or (loss). Subtract line 23 from line 19. If a related party exchange, see instructions   **24**

25   **Basis of like-kind property received.** Subtract line 15 from the sum of lines 18 and 23 . .   **25**

Part IV   **Deferral of Gain From Section 1043 Conflict-of-Interest Sales**

Note: *This part is to be used **only** by officers or employees of the executive branch of the Federal Government for reporting nonrecognition of gain under section 1043 on the sale of property to comply with the conflict-of-interest requirements. This part can be used **only** if the cost of the replacement property is more than the basis of the divested property.*

26   Enter the number from the upper right corner of your certificate of divestiture. (**Do not** attach a copy of your certificate. Keep the certificate with your records.). . . . . ▶ _____ – _____

27   Description of divested property ▶ _____

28   Description of replacement property ▶ _____

29   Date divested property was sold (month, day, year) . . . .   **29**   /   /

30   Sales price of divested property (see instructions) **30**

31   Basis of divested property **31**

32   **Realized gain.** Subtract line 31 from line 30 . . . .   **32**

33   Cost of replacement property purchased within 60 days after date of sale **33**

34   Subtract line 33 from line 30. If zero or less, enter -0- **34**

35   Ordinary income under recapture rules. Enter here and on Form 4797, line 10 (see instructions)   **35**

36   Subtract line 35 from line 34. If zero or less, enter -0-. If more than zero, enter here and on Schedule D or Form 4797 (see instructions) **36**

37   **Deferred gain.** Subtract the sum of lines 35 and 36 from line 32 . . . .   **37**

38   **Basis of replacement property.** Subtract line 37 from line 33 . . . .   **38**

Form **8824** (2006)

Figure 5.1 | Form 8824: Like-Kind Exchanges (continued)

Form 8824 (2006)   Page **3**

General Instructions

Section references are to the Internal Revenue Code unless otherwise noted.

Purpose of Form

Use Parts I, II, and III of Form 8824 to report each exchange of business or investment property for property of a like kind. Certain members of the executive branch of the Federal Government use Part IV to elect to defer gain on conflict-of-interest sales.

Multiple exchanges. If you made more than one like-kind exchange, you may file only a summary Form 8824 and attach your own statement showing all the information requested on Form 8824 for each exchange. Include your name and identifying number at the top of each page of the statement. On the summary Form 8824, enter only your name and identifying number, "Summary" on line 1, the total recognized gain from all exchanges on line 23, and the total basis of all like-kind property received on line 25.

When To File

If during the current tax year you transferred property to another party in a like-kind exchange, you must file Form 8824 with your tax return for that year. Also file Form 8824 for the 2 years following the year of a related party exchange (see the instructions for line 7 on page 4).

Like-Kind Exchanges

Generally, if you exchange business or investment property solely for business or investment property of a like kind, section 1031 provides that no gain or loss is recognized. If, as part of the exchange, you also receive other (not like-kind) property or money, gain is recognized to the extent of the other property and money received, but a loss is not recognized.

Section 1031 does not apply to exchanges of inventory, stocks, bonds, notes, other securities or evidence of indebtedness, or certain other assets. See section 1031(a)(2). In addition, section 1031 does not apply to certain exchanges involving tax-exempt use property subject to a lease. See section 470(e)(4).

Like-kind property. Properties are of like kind if they are of the same nature or character, even if they differ in grade or quality. Personal properties of a like class are like-kind properties. However, livestock of different sexes are not like-kind properties. Also, personal property used predominantly in the United States and personal property used predominantly outside the United States are not like-kind properties. See Pub. 544, Sales and Other Dispositions of Assets, for more details.

Real properties generally are of like kind, regardless of whether they are improved or unimproved. However, real property in the United States and real property outside the United States are not like-kind properties.

Deferred exchanges. A deferred exchange occurs when the property received in the exchange is received after the transfer of the property given up. For a deferred exchange to qualify as like-kind, you must comply with the 45-day written notice and receipt requirements explained in the instructions for lines 5 and 6.

Multi-asset exchanges. A multi-asset exchange involves the transfer and receipt of more than one group of like-kind properties. For example, an exchange of land, vehicles, and cash for land and vehicles is a multi-asset exchange. An exchange of land, vehicles, and cash for land only is not a multi-asset exchange. The transfer or receipt of multiple properties within one like-kind group is also a multi-asset exchange. Special rules apply when figuring the amount of gain recognized and your basis in properties received in a multi-asset exchange. For details, see Regulations section 1.1031(j)-1.

Reporting of multi-asset exchanges. If you transferred and received (a) more than one group of like-kind properties or (b) cash or other (not like-kind) property, do not complete lines 12 through 18 of Form 8824. Instead, attach your own statement showing how you figured the realized and recognized gain, and enter the correct amount on lines 19 through 25. Report any recognized gains on Schedule D; Form 4797, Sales of Business Property; or Form 6252, Installment Sale Income, whichever applies.

Exchanges using a qualified exchange accommodation arrangement (QEAA). If property is transferred to an exchange accommodation titleholder (EAT) and held in a QEAA, the EAT may be treated as the beneficial owner of the property, the property transferred from the EAT to you may be treated as property you received in an exchange, and the property you transferred to the EAT may be treated as property you gave up in an exchange. This may be true even if the property you are to receive is transferred to the EAT before you transfer the property you are giving up. However, the property transferred to you may not be treated as property received in an exchange if you previously owned it within 180 days of its transfer to the EAT. For details, see Rev. Proc. 2000-37 as modified by Rev. Proc. 2004-51. Rev. Proc. 2000-37 is on page 308 of Internal Revenue Bulletin 2000-40 at *www.irs.gov/pub/irs-irbs/irb00-40.pdf.* Rev. Proc. 2004-51 is on page 294 of Internal Revenue Bulletin 2004-33 at *www.irs.gov/irb/2004-33_IRB/ar13.html.*

Property used as home. If the property given up was owned and used as your home during the 5-year period ending on the date of the exchange, you may be able to exclude part or all of any gain figured on Form 8824. For details on the exclusion (including how to figure the amount of the exclusion), see Pub. 523, Selling Your Home. Fill out Form 8824 according to its instructions, with these exceptions:

1. Subtract line 18 from line 17. Subtract the amount of the exclusion from the result. Enter that result on line 19. On the dotted line next to line 19, enter "Section 121 exclusion" and the amount of the exclusion.

2. On line 20, enter the smaller of:
   a. Line 15 minus the exclusion, or
   b. Line 19.
   Do not enter less than zero.

3. Subtract line 15 from the sum of lines 18 and 23. Add the amount of your exclusion to the result. Enter that sum on line 25.

Property used partly as home. If the property given up was used partly as a home, you will need to use two separate Forms 8824 as worksheets—one for the part of the property used as a home and one for the part used for business or investment. Fill out only lines 15 through 25 of each worksheet Form 8824. On the worksheet Form 8824 for the part of property used as a home, follow steps (1) through (3) above, except that instead of following step (2), enter the amount from line 19 on line 20. On the worksheet Form 8824 for the part of the property used for business or investment, follow steps (1) through (3) above only if you can exclude at least part of any gain from the exchange of that part of the property; otherwise, complete the form according to its instructions. Enter the combined amounts from lines 15 through 25 of both worksheet Forms 8824 on the Form 8824 you file. Do not file either worksheet Form 8824.

More information. For details, see Rev. Proc. 2005-14 on page 528 of Internal Revenue Bulletin 2005-7 at *www.irs.gov/irb/2005-07_IRB/ar10.html.*

Additional information. For more information on like-kind exchanges, see section 1031 and its regulations and Pub. 544.

Specific Instructions

Lines 1 and 2. For real property, enter the address and type of property. For personal property, enter a short description. For property located outside the United States, include the country.

Line 5. Enter on line 5 the date of the written notice that identifies the like-kind property you received in a deferred exchange. To comply with the **45-day written notice requirement,** the following conditions must be met.

1. The like-kind property you receive in a deferred exchange must be designated in writing as replacement property either in a document you signed or in a written agreement signed by all parties to the exchange.

2. The document or agreement must describe the replacement property in a clear and recognizable manner. Real property should be described using a legal description, street address, or distinguishable name (for example, "Mayfair Apartment Building").

Figure 5.1 | Form 8824: Like-Kind Exchanges (continued)

3. No later than 45 days after the date you transferred the property you gave up:

a. You must send, fax, or hand deliver the document you signed to the person required to transfer the replacement property to you (including a disqualified person) or to another person involved in the exchange (other than a disqualified person), or

b. All parties to the exchange must sign the written agreement designating the replacement property.

Generally, a disqualified person is either your agent at the time of the transaction or a person related to you. For more details, see Regulations section 1.1031(k)-1(k).

Note. If you received the replacement property before the end of the 45-day period, you automatically are treated as having met the 45-day written notice requirement. In this case, enter on line 5 the date you received the replacement property.

Line 6. Enter on line 6 the date you received the like-kind property from the other party.

The property must be received by the earlier of the following dates.

• The 180th day after the date you transferred the property given up in the exchange.

• The due date (including extensions) of your tax return for the year in which you transferred the property given up.

Line 7. Special rules apply to like-kind exchanges made with related parties, either directly or indirectly. A **related party** includes your spouse, child, grandchild, parent, grandparent, brother, sister, or a related corporation, S corporation, partnership, trust, or estate. See section 1031(f).

An exchange made **indirectly** with a related party includes:

• An exchange made with a related party through an intermediary (such as a qualified intermediary or an exchange accommodation titleholder, as defined in Pub. 544), or

• An exchange made by a disregarded entity (such as a single member limited liability company) if you or a related party owned that entity.

If the related party (either directly or indirectly) or you dispose of the property received in an exchange before the date that is 2 years after the last transfer of property from the exchange, the deferred gain or (loss) from line 24 must be reported on your return for the year of disposition (unless an exception on line 11 applies).

If you are filing this form for 1 of the 2 years following the year of the exchange, complete Parts I and II. If both lines 9 and 10 are "No," **stop.**

If either line 9 or line 10 is "Yes," and an exception on line 11 applies, check the applicable box on line 11, attach any required explanation, and **stop.** If no line 11 exceptions apply, complete Part III.

Report the deferred gain or (loss) from line 24 on this year's tax return as if the exchange had been a sale.

An exchange structured to avoid the related party rules is not a like-kind exchange. Do not report it on Form 8824. Instead, you should report the disposition of the property given up as if the exchange had been a sale. See section 1031(f)(4). Such an exchange includes the transfer of property you gave up to a qualifed intermediary in exchange for property you received that was formerly owned by a related party if the related party received cash or other (not like-kind) property for the property you received, and you used the qualified intermediary to avoid the application of the related party rules. See Rev. Rul. 2002-83 for more details. You can find Rev. Rul. 2002-83 on page 927 of Internal Revenue Bulletin 2002-49 at *www.irs.gov/pub/irs-irbs/irb02-49.pdf.*

Line 11c. If you believe that you can establish to the satisfaction of the IRS that tax avoidance was not a principal purpose of both the exchange and the disposition, attach an explanation. Generally, tax avoidance will not be seen as a principal purpose in the case of:

• A disposition of property in a nonrecognition transaction,

• An exchange in which the related parties derive no tax advantage from the shifting of basis between the exchanged properties, or

• An exchange of undivided interests in different properties that results in each related party holding either the entire interest in a single property or a larger undivided interest in any of the properties.

Lines 12, 13, and 14. If you gave up other property in addition to the like-kind property, enter the fair market value (FMV) and the adjusted basis of the other property on lines 12 and 13, respectively. The gain or (loss) from this property is figured on line 14 and must be reported on your return. Report gain or (loss) as if the exchange were a sale.

Line 15. Include on line 15 the sum of:

• Any cash paid to you by the other party,

• The FMV of other (not like-kind) property you received, if any, and

• Net liabilities assumed by the other party—the excess, if any, of liabilities (including mortgages) assumed by the other party over the total of (a) any liabilities you assumed, (b) cash you paid to the other party, and (c) the FMV of the other (not like-kind) property you gave up.

Reduce the sum of the above amounts (but not below zero) by any exchange expenses you incurred. See the example on this page.

The following rules apply in determining the amount of liability treated as assumed.

• A recourse liability (or portion thereof) is treated as assumed by the party receiving the property if that party has agreed to and is expected to satisfy the liability (or portion thereof). It does not matter whether the party transferring the property has been relieved of the liability.

• A nonrecourse liability generally is treated as assumed by the party receiving the property subject to the liability. However, if an owner of other assets subject to the same liability agrees with the party receiving the property to, and is expected to, satisfy part or all of the liability, the amount treated as assumed is reduced by the smaller of (a) the amount of the liability that the owner of the other assets has agreed to and is expected to satisfy or (b) the FMV of those other assets.

Line 18. Include on line 18 the sum of:

• The adjusted basis of the like-kind property you gave up,

• Exchange expenses, if any (except for expenses used to reduce the amount reported on line 15), and

• Net amount paid to the other party—the **excess,** if any, of the total of (a) any liabilities you assumed, (b) cash you paid to the other party, and (c) the FMV of the other (not like-kind) property you gave up **over** any liabilities assumed by the other party.

See Regulations section 1.1031(d)-2 and the following example for figuring amounts to enter on lines 15 and 18.

Example. A owns an apartment house with an FMV of $220,000, an adjusted basis of $100,000, and subject to a mortgage of $80,000. B owns an apartment house with an FMV of $250,000, an adjusted basis of $175,000, and subject to a mortgage of $150,000.

A transfers his apartment house to B and receives in exchange B's apartment house plus $40,000 cash. A assumes the mortgage on the apartment house received from B, and B assumes the mortgage on the apartment house received from A.

A enters on line 15 only the $40,000 cash received from B. The $80,000 of liabilities assumed by B is not included because it does not exceed the $150,000 of liabilities A assumed. A enters $170,000 on line 18—the $100,000 adjusted basis, plus the $70,000 excess of the liabilities A assumed over the liabilities assumed by B ($150,000 - $80,000).

B enters $30,000 on line 15—the excess of the $150,000 of liabilities assumed by A over the total ($120,000) of the $80,000 of liabilities B assumed and the $40,000 cash B paid. B enters on line 18 only the adjusted basis of $175,000 because the total of the $80,000 of liabilities B assumed and the $40,000 cash B paid does not exceed the $150,000 of liabilities assumed by A.

Line 21. If you disposed of section 1245, 1250, 1252, 1254, or 1255 property (see the instructions for Part III of Form 4797), you may be required to recapture as ordinary income part or all of the realized gain (line 19). Figure the amount to enter on line 21 as follows:

Section 1245 property. Enter the smaller of:

1. The total adjustments for deductions (whether for the same or other property) allowed or allowable to you or any other

Figure 5.1 | Form 8824: Like-Kind Exchanges (continued)

person for depreciation or amortization (up to the amount of gain shown on line 19), or

2. The gain shown on line 20, if any, plus the FMV of non-section 1245 like-kind property received.

Section 1250 property. Enter the smaller of:

1. The gain you would have had to report as ordinary income because of additional depreciation if you had sold the property (see the Form 4797 instructions for line 26), or

2. The larger of:

a. The gain shown on line 20, if any, or

b. The excess, if any, of the gain in item (1) above over the FMV of the section 1250 property received.

Section 1252, 1254, and 1255 property. The rules for these types of property are similar to those for section 1245 property. See Regulations section 1.1252-2(d) and Temporary Regulations section 16A.1255-2(c) for details. If the installment method applies to this exchange:

1. See section 453(f)(6) to determine the installment sale income taxable for this year and report it on Form 6252.

2. Enter on Form 6252, line 25 or 36, the section 1252, 1254, or 1255 recapture amount you figured on Form 8824, line 21. Do not enter more than the amount shown on Form 6252, line 24 or 35.

3. Also enter this amount on Form 4797, line 15.

4. If all the ordinary income is not recaptured this year, report in future years on Form 6252 the ordinary income up to the taxable installment sale income, until it is all reported.

Line 22. Report a gain from the exchange of property used in a trade or business (and other noncapital assets) on Form 4797, line 5 or line 16. Report a gain from the exchange of capital assets according to the Schedule D instructions for your return. Be sure to use the date of the exchange as the date for reporting the gain. If the installment method applies to this exchange, see section 453(f)(6) to determine the installment sale income taxable for this year and report it on Form 6252.

Line 24. If line 19 is a loss, enter it on line 24. Otherwise, subtract the amount on line 23 from the amount on line 19 and enter the result. For exchanges with related parties, see the instructions for line 7 on page 4.

Line 25. The amount on line 25 is your basis in the like-kind property you received in the exchange. Your basis in other property received in the exchange, if any, is its FMV.

Section 1043 Conflict-of-Interest Sales (Part IV)

If you sell property at a gain according to a certificate of divestiture issued by the Office of Government Ethics (OGE) and purchase replacement property (permitted property), you may elect to defer part or all of the realized gain. You must recognize gain on the sale only to the extent that the amount realized on the sale is more than the cost of replacement property purchased within 60 days after the sale. (You also must recognize any ordinary income recapture.) Permitted property is any obligation of the United States or any diversified investment fund approved by the OGE.

 If the property you sold was stock you acquired by exercising a statutory stock option, you may be treated as meeting the holding periods that apply to such stock, regardless of how long you actually held the stock. This may benefit you if you do not defer your entire gain, because it may allow you to treat the gain as a capital gain instead of ordinary income. For details, see section 421(d) or Pub. 525.

Complete Part IV of Form 8824 only if the cost of the replacement property is more than the basis of the divested property and you elect to defer the gain. Otherwise, report the sale on Schedule D or Form 4797, whichever applies.

Your basis in the replacement property is reduced by the amount of the deferred gain. If you made more than one purchase of replacement property, reduce your basis in the replacement property in the order you acquired it.

Line 30. Enter the amount you received from the sale of the divested property, minus any selling expenses.

Line 35. Follow these steps to determine the amount to enter.

1. Use Part III of Form 4797 as a worksheet to figure ordinary income under the recapture rules.

2. Enter on Form 8824, line 35, the amount from Form 4797, line 31. Do not attach the Form 4797 used as a worksheet to your return.

3. Report the amount from line 35 on Form 4797, line 10, column (g). In column (a), write "From Form 8824, line 35." Do not complete columns (b) through (f).

Line 36. If you sold a capital asset, enter any capital gain from line 36 on Schedule D. If you sold property used in a trade or business (or any other asset for which the gain is treated as ordinary income), report the gain on Form 4797, line 2 or line 10, column (g). In column (a), write "From Form 8824, line 36." Do not complete columns (b) through (f).

Paperwork Reduction Act Notice. We ask for the information on this form to carry out the Internal Revenue laws of the United States. You are required to give us the information. We need it to ensure that you are complying with these laws and to allow us to figure and collect the right amount of tax.

You are not required to provide the information requested on a form that is subject to the Paperwork Reduction Act unless the form displays a valid OMB control number. Books or records relating to a form or its instructions must be retained as long as their contents may become material in the administration of any Internal Revenue law. Generally, tax returns and return information are confidential, as required by section 6103.

The time needed to complete and file this form will vary depending on individual circumstances. The estimated burden for individual taxpayers filing this form is approved under OMB control number 1545-0074 and is included in the estimates shown in the instructions for their individual income tax return. The estimated burden for all other taxpayers who file this form is shown below.

Recordkeeping . . . . 1 hr., 38 min.

Learning about the law or the form . . . . 27 min.

Preparing the form . . . . . 59 min.

Copying, assembling, and sending the form to the IRS . . 33 min.

If you have comments concerning the accuracy of these time estimates or suggestions for making this form simpler, we would be happy to hear from you. See the instructions for the tax return with which this form is filed.

Figure 5.2 | Exchange Agreement

STATE OF NORTH CAROLINA
COUNTY OF ORANGE   **EXCHANGE AGREEMENT**

    THIS EXCHANGE AGREEMENT ("Exchange Agreement"), made and entered into as of _____, by and between _____ ("Transferor"); and Investors Title Exchange Corporation, a North Carolina corporation ("ITEC");

            W I T N E S S E T H:

    WHEREAS, Transferor owns certain real property located in the City of _____, _____ County, _____, which real property is more particularly described on Exhibit A attached hereto and incorporated herein by reference (the "Relinquished Property"); and

    WHEREAS, Transferor intends to exchange the Relinquished Property for other real property or properties of like kind (the "Replacement Property") pursuant to Section 1031 of the Internal Revenue Code of 1986, as amended (the "Code"); and

    WHEREAS, ITEC for a fee has agreed to act as a qualified intermediary pursuant to Section 1031 of the Code and Treasury Regulations promulgated thereunder in order to facilitate Transferor's exchange.

    NOW THEREFORE, for and in consideration of the mutual covenants and agreements herein contained, the parties to this Exchange Agreement hereby do agree as follows:

    1. Exchange of Properties: Pursuant to this Exchange Agreement, ITEC shall acquire the Relinquished Property from Transferor, transfer the Relinquished Property, acquire the Replacement Property, and transfer the Replacement Property to Transferor. The transfer of the Replacement Property to Transferor may be simultaneous with, or may occur subsequent to, the acquisition of the Relinquished Property from Transferor.

    2. Transfer of Relinquished Property: Transferor shall enter into a contract to sell the Relinquished Property to a "Third-Party Buyer," which contract shall be referred to herein as the "Sales Contract." The Sales Contract shall be assignable and shall contain such terms and conditions as may be reasonably acceptable to ITEC. On or before closing, Transferor shall assign Transferor's rights, title, and interests in the Sales Contract to ITEC (the "Relinquished Property Assignment"). ITEC may authorize Transferor to convey title directly to Third-Party Buyer at closing. The Exchange Balance, as defined in Section 3 below, shall be paid to and held by ITEC upon the closing of the Relinquished Property transfer.

    3. Exchange Balance: For purposes of this Exchange Agreement, the "Exchange Balance" is the purchase price for the Relinquished Property set forth in the Sales Contract reduced by the following:

      a. transactional items that relate to the disposition of the Relinquished Property and appear under local standards in typical closing statements as the responsibility of a seller, including without limitation, ITEC's fee (if not otherwise paid by Transferor),

Figure 5.2 | Exchange Agreement (continued)

b. the amount of all principal and accrued interest on any obligation (including any associated prepayment penalty) secured by the Relinquished Property that is not paid directly by Transferor on or before the closing, and

c. any boot that Transferor receives from the Third-Party Buyer of the Relinquished Property.

4. <u>Growth Factor</u>: ITEC shall pay Transferor interest on the Exchange Balance at the rate of _____% per annum, calculated on the lowest Exchange Balance for each calendar month. All such interest shall be subject to the restrictions set forth in Section 8 below, and shall be attributable to Transferor as interest income for income tax purposes. Transferor shall complete the Internal Revenue Service Form W-9 attached as Exhibit B to this Exchange Agreement.

5. <u>Identification of Replacement Property</u>: Transferor shall identify the Replacement Property by giving written notice thereof to ITEC using the Replacement Property Identification Form attached as Exhibit C hereto. Identification shall be made within the period beginning on the date of transfer of the first Relinquished Property and ending at midnight on the 45th calendar day thereafter (the "Identification Period"). The Replacement Property Identification Form must be signed by Transferor and either hand delivered, mailed, telecopied or otherwise delivered to ITEC within the Identification Period. Transferor shall have sole responsibility for timely and appropriately identifying Replacement Property.

6. <u>Exchange Period</u>: Provided that Transferor has properly identified Replacement Property, the closing of the Replacement Property shall occur within the Exchange Period (defined below). For purposes of this Exchange Agreement, "Exchange Period" is the period of time that begins on the date of the transfer of the first Relinquished Property and ends at midnight on the earlier of:

a. the 180th calendar day thereafter; or

b. the due date of Transferor's federal income tax return (including extensions) for Transferor's tax return for the year in which the closing on the Relinquished Property occurs. If a filing extension applies to the deadline, the Transferor must notify ITEC in writing.

7. <u>Transfer of Replacement Property</u>: Transferor shall enter into a contract to purchase the Replacement Property with a "Third-Party Seller," which contract shall be referred to herein as the "Purchase Contract." The Purchase Contract shall be assignable and shall contain such terms and conditions as may be reasonably acceptable to ITEC. Transferor shall assign Transferor's rights, title, and interests in the Purchase Contract to ITEC (the "Replacement Property Assignment"). Pursuant to the Purchase Contract and Replacement Property Assignment, ITEC shall pay the Exchange Balance towards the acquisition of the Replacement Property, including payment for transactional items that relate to the acquisition of the Replacement Property and appear under local standards in typical closing statements as the responsibility of a buyer. Transferor shall be responsible for designating a closing attorney or settlement agent (the "Settlement Agent").

2

Figure 5.2 | Exchange Agreement (continued)

Transferor shall provide ITEC with written contact information for the Settlement Agent by either, (i) designating the Settlement Agent in the Purchase Contact, or (ii) utilizing Exhibit D attached hereto (the "Settlement Agent Designation Form"). ITEC shall then be authorized to disburse all or a portion of the Exchange Balance to the designated Settlement Agent for the Replacement Property closing.

In no event will ITEC be required to expend more than the Exchange Balance for the acquisition of the Replacement Property. Accordingly, if the total costs for the acquisition of the Replacement Property pursuant to the Purchase Contract are greater than the amount of the Exchange Balance held by ITEC as of the date of the closing of the Replacement Property, Transferor shall be responsible for the excess at the closing of the Replacement Property. Any of the Exchange Balance not expended by ITEC at the closing of the Replacement Property shall be paid to Transferor subject to the restrictions set forth in Section 8 below, and may cause the exchange contemplated herein to be partially taxable to Transferor.

8. <u>Transferor's Right to Demand Exchange Balance and Restrictions on Exchange Balance</u>: Transferor shall have no right to receive, pledge, borrow or otherwise obtain the benefits of the Exchange Balance held by ITEC until after the end of the Exchange Period; provided, however, upon the occurrence of the earliest of any of the events set forth below, Transferor may request in writing that ITEC pay any remaining Exchange Balance to Transferor:

a. At midnight on the last day of the Identification Period if Transferor then has not identified any Replacement Property; or

b. At midnight on the last day of the Exchange Period, if Transferor identifies Replacement Property within the Identification Period, but title to the Replacement Property has not then been transferred to Transferor within the Exchange Period; or

c. At such time as when title to all Replacement Property, which Transferor has timely identified pursuant to this Exchange Agreement, has been transferred to Transferor.

9. <u>ITEC's Fee</u>: ITEC's base fee for acting as qualified intermediary hereunder is the sum of $600.00, due and payable upon the first Relinquished Property transfer. If more than three properties are facilitated under this Exchange Agreement, an additional fee of $200.00 per property will be due to ITEC upon each additional transfer. There shall also be an administrative fee of $20.00 for each wire transfer of funds or overnight delivery of documents sent by ITEC. In the event that no Relinquished Property transfer contemplated under this Exchange Agreement occurs, a $100.00 document preparation/cancellation fee shall be due. ITEC may deduct any unpaid fees from the Exchange Balance at the time the fees are incurred.

10. <u>ITEC's Responsibilities</u>: ITEC reserves the right to review the Sales Contract and Purchase Contracts only for purposes of determining whether ITEC will accept the assignment of Transferor's rights, title, and interests therein. ITEC shall not be required to disburse any funds from the Exchange Balance pursuant to its obligations under this Exchange Agreement without advance written notice of at least 3 business days.

3

Figure 5.2 | Exchange Agreement (continued)

11.   Termination of Exchange Agreement: This Exchange Agreement shall terminate upon the 30th day after an event giving rise to Transferor's right to demand the Exchange Balance set forth in Section 8 hereof. Within 5 business days following termination as hereinabove provided, any remaining Exchange Balance shall be paid by ITEC To Transferor.

12.   Allocation of Liability:
a.   Transferor represents and warrants that all information and data which Transferor has provided to ITEC regarding the Relinquished Property or Replacement Property is true and accurate, except where Transferor has indicated to ITEC that such information and data is true and accurate only to Transferor's belief.

b.   Transferor represents and warrants that except as disclosed in an Exhibit hereto, the Relinquished Property, the Replacement Property and Transferor's activities thereon comply with all applicable laws and regulations.

c.   Transferor represents and warrants that Transferor has obtained competent, independent legal and tax advice regarding the contemplated like-kind exchange and regarding this Exchange Agreement, the Sales Contract(s), Relinquished Property Assignment(s), Purchase Contract(s), Replacement Property Assignment(s), Settlement Statements, and related deeds for real property, and any and all other documents or agreements referred to herein or entered into in connection herewith ("Related Agreements"), and Transferor has not relied upon any statement or representation made by ITEC regarding the legal or tax implications of the transactions contemplated in this Exchange Agreement.

d.   ITEC makes no representations or warranties that the transaction contemplated in this Exchange Agreement qualifies as a like-kind exchange pursuant to Section 1031 of the Code and has tendered to Transferor no legal, tax or business advice in connection with the Related Agreements.

e.   Absent gross negligence or willful misconduct by ITEC, Transferor releases ITEC from all Claims and costs arising from (i) ITEC's acts or omissions in connection with the Related Agreements, (ii) the failure of Relinquished Property to close in a timely fashion, (iii) the failure of Transferor to locate or properly identify appropriate Replacement Property within the Identification Period, (iv) the failure of the Relinquished Property or Replacement Property to qualify as like-kind exchange property within the meaning of Section 1031 of the Code, (v) if Transferor has properly identified Replacement Property within the Identification Period, the failure of Replacement Property to close within the Exchange Period, (vi) the failure for any reason of the exchange of the Relinquished Property for the Replacement Property by Transferor to qualify as a like-kind exchange pursuant to Section 1031 of the Code, (vii) any loss or impairment of funds while on deposit with a federally insured banking institution resulting from failure, bankruptcy, insolvency or suspension of such institution, and (viii) any loss or impairment of funds while in the possession of designated Settlement Agent.

13.   Indemnity and Compliance with Laws: For purposes of this Exchange Agreement, "Claim" means administrative, regulatory or judicial action, suit, liability, judgment, penalty, damages, directive, order or claim; and "Indemnify" means to indemnify, defend and reimburse the indemnitee and its successors and assigns on an after-tax basis.

4

Figure 5.2 | Exchange Agreement (continued)

a.   Transferor shall Indemnify ITEC against any Claims and costs (including reasonable litigation expenses) arising from the Related Agreements or any environmental or other conditions on the Relinquished Property or the Replacement Property.

b.   ITEC shall notify Transferor promptly upon learning of a Claim or cost subject to indemnification under this Exchange Agreement. ITEC shall cooperate with Transferor in the defense of such Claim, but shall not be obligated to defend such Claim or pay the costs of doing so.

c.   Transferor shall comply with all laws, regulations and orders of public authorities regarding the Relinquished Property and the Replacement Property at all times when ITEC is acting as qualified intermediary with respect to said properties pursuant to this Exchange Agreement.

14.   Litigation Expenses: In the event ITEC institutes litigation or any other dispute resolution action (including without limitation, arbitration or mediation) against Transferor for any reason in connection with this Exchange Agreement, Transferor shall pay all costs and expenses, including without limitation attorneys' fees, incurred by ITEC in such action.

15.   Default and Remedies: In the event ITEC breaches this Exchange Agreement, Transferor's exclusive remedy shall be to terminate this Exchange Agreement, to receive the Exchange Balance and to receive a refund of $600.00 as liquidated damages. Transferor waives any other rights or remedies except as to Claims for which ITEC may be held liable to Transferor under Section 12 above. In the event Transferor breaches this Exchange Agreement, ITEC may pursue any remedies available under this Exchange Agreement and at law and equity.

16.   Entire Understanding: This Exchange Agreement constitutes the entire understanding between the parties. It may be modified only by a writing signed by the parties hereto. No term or provision hereof shall be deemed waived and no breach excused except by written consent.

17.   Duplicate Originals: The parties to this Exchange Agreement may execute this Exchange Agreement or Related Agreements in duplicate originals, or by facsimile copy if desired, each of which when so executed shall be deemed to be an original, and all of which taken together shall constitute one and the same agreement, binding upon all parties hereto.

18.   Notices: All notices required or permitted to be given under the terms of this Exchange Agreement shall be considered properly made if personally delivered or sent by certified mail, return-receipt requested, postage prepaid, to the parties at the addresses set forth below:

Transferor:

5

Figure 5.2 | Exchange Agreement (continued)

Copy to:

ITEC: Investors Title Exchange Corporation
                         Post Office Drawer 2687
                         Chapel Hill, North Carolina 27514
                         Attn:

19.   Applicable Law: This Exchange Agreement shall be governed by North Carolina law. Any suit or action related to this Exchange Agreement shall be prosecuted in the courts of the County of Orange, State of North Carolina.

20.   Binding Effect; Assignment: This Exchange Agreement shall be binding upon and inure to the benefit of ITEC, and its respective successors and assigns. Neither ITEC nor Transferor shall assign this Exchange Agreement to any other person or entity without the prior written consent of the other party to this Exchange Agreement.

21.   Time: Time is of the essence in this Exchange Agreement.

22.   Survival: The representations and warranties made by or on behalf of Transferor contained in this Exchange Agreement or in any document referred to herein or in connection with the transactions contemplated herein, and the obligation of Transferor to provide indemnification as set forth in Section 13 hereof, shall survive the termination of this Exchange Agreement and the closing of the Relinquished Property and the Replacement Property as herein provided.

23.   Severability: The invalidity or unenforceability of any provision of this Exchange Agreement shall not affect the validity or enforceability of any other provision.

24.   Third Parties: Except as otherwise provided herein, this Exchange Agreement grants no rights or remedies to any parties other than Transferor and ITEC.

25.   Transferor is Not a Foreign Person: Transferor hereby certifies, under penalty of perjury, that Transferor is not a "foreign person" as defined by Section 1445 of the Internal Revenue Code and the Treasury Regulations promulgated thereunder.

26.   Exhibits: The Exhibits attached hereto are incorporated by reference.

(Signature Page Follows)

6

Figure 5.2 | Exchange Agreement (continued)

IN WITNESS WHEREOF, the parties hereto have caused this Exchange Agreement to be executed under seal and in such form as to be binding, on the day and year first above written.

ITEC: Investors Title Exchange Corporation,
                   a North Carolina corporation

By:_____
Name:
Title:

TRANSFEROR: _____

                   _____

7

Figure 5.3 | Exhibit A

EXHIBIT A

<u>Relinquished Property Description</u>

All that certain real property situated in the City of _____, _____
County, _____, and Being:

Figure 5.4 | Exhibit B

Form **W-9** (Rev. November 2005) Department of the Treasury Internal Revenue Service	**Request for Taxpayer Identification Number and Certification**	Give form to the requester. Do not send to the IRS.

Print or type   See Specific Instructions on page 2.

Name (as shown on your income tax return)

Business name, if different from above

Check appropriate box: ☐ Individual/ Sole proprietor   ☐ Corporation   ☐ Partnership   ☐ Other ▶ ....   ☐ Exempt from backup withholding

Address (number, street, and apt. or suite no.)

Requester's name and address (optional)

City, state, and ZIP code

List account number(s) here (optional)

Part I **Taxpayer Identification Number (TIN)**

Enter your TIN in the appropriate box. The TIN provided must match the name given on Line 1 to avoid backup withholding. For individuals, this is your social security number (SSN). However, for a resident alien, sole proprietor, or disregarded entity, see the Part I instructions on page 3. For other entities, it is your employer identification number (EIN). If you do not have a number, see *How to get a TIN* on page 3.

Note. If the account is in more than one name, see the chart on page 4 for guidelines on whose number to enter.

Social security number

or

Employer identification number

Part II **Certification**

Under penalties of perjury, I certify that:

1. The number shown on this form is my correct taxpayer identification number (or I am waiting for a number to be issued to me), and

2. I am not subject to backup withholding because: (a) I am exempt from backup withholding, or (b) I have not been notified by the Internal Revenue Service (IRS) that I am subject to backup withholding as a result of a failure to report all interest or dividends, or (c) the IRS has notified me that I am no longer subject to backup withholding, and

3. I am a U.S. person (including a U.S. resident alien).

Certification instructions. You must cross out item 2 above if you have been notified by the IRS that you are currently subject to backup withholding because you have failed to report all interest and dividends on your tax return. For real estate transactions, item 2 does not apply. For mortgage interest paid, acquisition or abandonment of secured property, cancellation of debt, contributions to an individual retirement arrangement (IRA), and generally, payments other than interest and dividends, you are not required to sign the Certification, but you must provide your correct TIN. (See the instructions on page 4.)

Sign Here   Signature of U.S. person ▶   Date ▶

Purpose of Form

A person who is required to file an information return with the IRS, must obtain your correct taxpayer identification number (TIN) to report, for example, income paid to you, real estate transactions, mortgage interest you paid, acquisition or abandonment of secured property, cancellation of debt, or contributions you made to an IRA.

U.S. person. Use Form W-9 only if you are a U.S. person (including a resident alien), to provide your correct TIN to the person requesting it (the requester) and, when applicable, to:

   1. Certify that the TIN you are giving is correct (or you are waiting for a number to be issued),

   2. Certify that you are not subject to backup withholding, or

   3. Claim exemption from backup withholding if you are a U.S. exempt payee.

   In 3 above, if applicable, you are also certifying that as a U.S. person, your allocable share of any partnership income from a U.S. trade or business is not subject to the withholding tax on foreign partners' share of effectively connected income.

Note. If a requester gives you a form other than Form W-9 to request your TIN, you must use the requester's form if it is substantially similar to this Form W-9.

   For federal tax purposes, you are considered a person if you are:

● An individual who is a citizen or resident of the United States,

● A partnership, corporation, company, or association created or organized in the United States or under the laws of the United States, or

● Any estate (other than a foreign estate) or trust. See Regulations sections 301.7701-6(a) and 7(a) for additional information.

Special rules for partnerships. Partnerships that conduct a trade or business in the United States are generally required to pay a withholding tax on any foreign partners' share of income from such business. Further, in certain cases where a Form W-9 has not been received, a partnership is required to presume that a partner is a foreign person, and pay the withholding tax. Therefore, if you are a U.S. person that is a partner in a partnership conducting a trade or business in the United States, provide Form W-9 to the partnership to establish your U.S. status and avoid withholding on your share of partnership income.

   The person who gives Form W-9 to the partnership for purposes of establishing its U.S. status and avoiding withholding on its allocable share of net income from the partnership conducting a trade or business in the United States is in the following cases:

● The U.S. owner of a disregarded entity and not the entity,

Cat. No. 10231X   Form **W-9** (Rev. 11-2005)

Figure 5.4 | Exhibit B (continued)

● The U.S. grantor or other owner of a grantor trust and not the trust, and

● The U.S. trust (other than a grantor trust) and not the beneficiaries of the trust.

Foreign person. If you are a foreign person, do not use Form W-9. Instead, use the appropriate Form W-8 (see Publication 515, Withholding of Tax on Nonresident Aliens and Foreign Entities).

Nonresident alien who becomes a resident alien. Generally, only a nonresident alien individual may use the terms of a tax treaty to reduce or eliminate U.S. tax on certain types of income. However, most tax treaties contain a provision known as a "saving clause." Exceptions specified in the saving clause may permit an exemption from tax to continue for certain types of income even after the recipient has otherwise become a U.S. resident alien for tax purposes.

If you are a U.S. resident alien who is relying on an exception contained in the saving clause of a tax treaty to claim an exemption from U.S. tax on certain types of income, you must attach a statement to Form W-9 that specifies the following five items:

1. The treaty country. Generally, this must be the same treaty under which you claimed exemption from tax as a nonresident alien.

2. The treaty article addressing the income.

3. The article number (or location) in the tax treaty that contains the saving clause and its exceptions.

4. The type and amount of income that qualifies for the exemption from tax.

5. Sufficient facts to justify the exemption from tax under the terms of the treaty article.

Example. Article 20 of the U.S.-China income tax treaty allows an exemption from tax for scholarship income received by a Chinese student temporarily present in the United States. Under U.S. law, this student will become a resident alien for tax purposes if his or her stay in the United States exceeds 5 calendar years. However, paragraph 2 of the first Protocol to the U.S.-China treaty (dated April 30, 1984) allows the provisions of Article 20 to continue to apply even after the Chinese student becomes a resident alien of the United States. A Chinese student who qualifies for this exception (under paragraph 2 of the first protocol) and is relying on this exception to claim an exemption from tax on his or her scholarship or fellowship income would attach to Form W-9 a statement that includes the information described above to support that exemption.

If you are a nonresident alien or a foreign entity not subject to backup withholding, give the requester the appropriate completed Form W-8.

What is backup withholding? Persons making certain payments to you must under certain conditions withhold and pay to the IRS 28% of such payments (after December 31, 2002). This is called "backup withholding." Payments that may be subject to backup withholding include interest, dividends, broker and barter exchange transactions, rents, royalties, nonemployee pay, and certain payments from fishing boat operators. Real estate transactions are not subject to backup withholding.

You will not be subject to backup withholding on payments you receive if you give the requester your correct TIN, make the proper certifications, and report all your taxable interest and dividends on your tax return.

Payments you receive will be subject to backup withholding if:

1. You do not furnish your TIN to the requester,

2. You do not certify your TIN when required (see the Part II instructions on page 4 for details),

3. The IRS tells the requester that you furnished an incorrect TIN,

4. The IRS tells you that you are subject to backup withholding because you did not report all your interest and dividends on your tax return (for reportable interest and dividends only), or

5. You do not certify to the requester that you are not subject to backup withholding under 4 above (for reportable interest and dividend accounts opened after 1983 only).

Certain payees and payments are exempt from backup withholding. See the instructions below and the separate Instructions for the Requester of Form W-9.

Also see *Special rules regarding partnerships* on page 1.

Penalties

Failure to furnish TIN. If you fail to furnish your correct TIN to a requester, you are subject to a penalty of $50 for each such failure unless your failure is due to reasonable cause and not to willful neglect.

Civil penalty for false information with respect to withholding. If you make a false statement with no reasonable basis that results in no backup withholding, you are subject to a $500 penalty.

Criminal penalty for falsifying information. Willfully falsifying certifications or affirmations may subject you to criminal penalties including fines and/or imprisonment.

Misuse of TINs. If the requester discloses or uses TINs in violation of federal law, the requester may be subject to civil and criminal penalties.

Specific Instructions

Name

If you are an individual, you must generally enter the name shown on your income tax return. However, if you have changed your last name, for instance, due to marriage without informing the Social Security Administration of the name change, enter your first name, the last name shown on your social security card, and your new last name.

If the account is in joint names, list first, and then circle, the name of the person or entity whose number you entered in Part I of the form.

Sole proprietor. Enter your individual name as shown on your income tax return on the "Name" line. You may enter your business, trade, or "doing business as (DBA)" name on the "Business name" line.

Limited liability company (LLC). If you are a single-member LLC (including a foreign LLC with a domestic owner) that is disregarded as an entity separate from its owner under Treasury regulations section 301.7701-3, enter the owner's name on the "Name" line. Enter the LLC's name on the "Business name" line. Check the appropriate box for your filing status (sole proprietor, corporation, etc.), then check the box for "Other" and enter "LLC" in the space provided.

Other entities. Enter your business name as shown on required federal tax documents on the "Name" line. This name should match the name shown on the charter or other legal document creating the entity. You may enter any business, trade, or DBA name on the "Business name" line.

Note. You are requested to check the appropriate box for your status (individual/sole proprietor, corporation, etc.).

Exempt From Backup Withholding

If you are exempt, enter your name as described above and check the appropriate box for your status, then check the "Exempt from backup withholding" box in the line following the business name, sign and date the form.

Figure 5.4 | Exhibit B (continued)

Generally, individuals (including sole proprietors) are not exempt from backup withholding. Corporations are exempt from backup withholding for certain payments, such as interest and dividends.

Note. If you are exempt from backup withholding, you should still complete this form to avoid possible erroneous backup withholding.

Exempt payees. Backup withholding is not required on any payments made to the following payees:

1. An organization exempt from tax under section 501(a), any IRA, or a custodial account under section 403(b)(7) if the account satisfies the requirements of section 401(f)(2),

2. The United States or any of its agencies or instrumentalities,

3. A state, the District of Columbia, a possession of the United States, or any of their political subdivisions or instrumentalities,

4. A foreign government or any of its political subdivisions, agencies, or instrumentalities, or

5. An international organization or any of its agencies or instrumentalities.

Other payees that may be exempt from backup withholding include:

6. A corporation,

7. A foreign central bank of issue,

8. A dealer in securities or commodities required to register in the United States, the District of Columbia, or a possession of the United States,

9. A futures commission merchant registered with the Commodity Futures Trading Commission,

10. A real estate investment trust,

11. An entity registered at all times during the tax year under the Investment Company Act of 1940,

12. A common trust fund operated by a bank under section 584(a),

13. A financial institution,

14. A middleman known in the investment community as a nominee or custodian, or

15. A trust exempt from tax under section 664 or described in section 4947.

The chart below shows types of payments that may be exempt from backup withholding. The chart applies to the exempt recipients listed above, 1 through 15.

IF the payment is for . . .	THEN the payment is exempt for . . .
Interest and dividend payments	All exempt recipients except for 9
Broker transactions	Exempt recipients 1 through 13. Also, a person registered under the Investment Advisers Act of 1940 who regularly acts as a broker
Barter exchange transactions and patronage dividends	Exempt recipients 1 through 5
Payments over $600 required to be reported and direct sales over $5,000 [1]	Generally, exempt recipients 1 through 7 [2]

[1] See Form 1099-MISC, Miscellaneous Income, and its instructions.

[2] However, the following payments made to a corporation (including gross proceeds paid to an attorney under section 6045(f), even if the attorney is a corporation) and reportable on Form 1099-MISC are not exempt from backup withholding: medical and health care payments, attorneys' fees; and payments for services paid by a federal executive agency.

Part I. Taxpayer Identification Number (TIN)

Enter your TIN in the appropriate box. If you are a resident alien and you do not have and are not eligible to get an SSN, your TIN is your IRS individual taxpayer identification number (ITIN). Enter it in the social security number box. If you do not have an ITIN, see *How to get a TIN* below.

If you are a sole proprietor and you have an EIN, you may enter either your SSN or EIN. However, the IRS prefers that you use your SSN.

If you are a single-owner LLC that is disregarded as an entity separate from its owner (see *Limited liability company (LLC)* on page 2), enter your SSN (or EIN, if you have one). If the LLC is a corporation, partnership, etc., enter the entity's EIN.

Note. See the chart on page 4 for further clarification of name and TIN combinations.

How to get a TIN. If you do not have a TIN, apply for one immediately. To apply for an SSN, get Form SS-5, Application for a Social Security Card, from your local Social Security Administration office or get this form online at *www.socialsecurity.gov*. You may also get this form by calling 1-800-772-1213. Use Form W-7, Application for IRS Individual Taxpayer Identification Number, to apply for an ITIN, or Form SS-4, Application for Employer Identification Number, to apply for an EIN. You can apply for an EIN online by accessing the IRS website at *www.irs.gov/businesses* and clicking on Employer ID Numbers under Related Topics. You can get Forms W-7 and SS-4 from the IRS by visiting *www.irs.gov* or by calling 1-800-TAX-FORM (1-800-829-3676).

If you are asked to complete Form W-9 but do not have a TIN, write "Applied For" in the space for the TIN, sign and date the form, and give it to the requester. For interest and dividend payments, and certain payments made with respect to readily tradable instruments, generally you will have 60 days to get a TIN and give it to the requester before you are subject to backup withholding on payments. The 60-day rule does not apply to other types of payments. You will be subject to backup withholding on all such payments until you provide your TIN to the requester.

Note. Writing "Applied For" means that you have already applied for a TIN or that you intend to apply for one soon.

Caution: *A disregarded domestic entity that has a foreign owner must use the appropriate Form W-8.*

Figure 5.4 | Exhibit B (continued)

Part II. Certification

To establish to the withholding agent that you are a U.S. person, or resident alien, sign Form W-9. You may be requested to sign by the withholding agent even if items 1, 4, and 5 below indicate otherwise.

For a joint account, only the person whose TIN is shown in Part I should sign (when required). Exempt recipients, see *Exempt From Backup Withholding* on page 2.

Signature requirements. Complete the certification as indicated in 1 through 5 below.

1. Interest, dividend, and barter exchange accounts opened before 1984 and broker accounts considered active during 1983. You must give your correct TIN, but you do not have to sign the certification.

2. Interest, dividend, broker, and barter exchange accounts opened after 1983 and broker accounts considered inactive during 1983. You must sign the certification or backup withholding will apply. If you are subject to backup withholding and you are merely providing your correct TIN to the requester, you must cross out item 2 in the certification before signing the form.

3. Real estate transactions. You must sign the certification. You may cross out item 2 of the certification.

4. Other payments. You must give your correct TIN, but you do not have to sign the certification unless you have been notified that you have previously given an incorrect TIN. "Other payments" include payments made in the course of the requester's trade or business for rents, royalties, goods (other than bills for merchandise), medical and health care services (including payments to corporations), payments to a nonemployee for services, payments to certain fishing boat crew members and fishermen, and gross proceeds paid to attorneys (including payments to corporations).

5. Mortgage interest paid by you, acquisition or abandonment of secured property, cancellation of debt, qualified tuition program payments (under section 529), IRA, Coverdell ESA, Archer MSA or HSA contributions or distributions, and pension distributions. You must give your correct TIN, but you do not have to sign the certification.

What Name and Number To Give the Requester

For this type of account:	Give name and SSN of:
1. Individual	The individual
2. Two or more individuals (joint account)	The actual owner of the account or, if combined funds, the first individual on the account [1]
3. Custodian account of a minor (Uniform Gift to Minors Act)	The minor [2]
4. a. The usual revocable savings trust (grantor is also trustee)	The grantor-trustee [1]
b. So-called trust account that is not a legal or valid trust under state law	The actual owner [1]
5. Sole proprietorship or single-owner LLC	The owner [3]

For this type of account:	Give name and EIN of:
6. Sole proprietorship or single-owner LLC	The owner [3]
7. A valid trust, estate, or pension trust	Legal entity [4]
8. Corporate or LLC electing corporate status on Form 8832	The corporation
9. Association, club, religious, charitable, educational, or other tax-exempt organization	The organization
10. Partnership or multi-member LLC	The partnership
11. A broker or registered nominee	The broker or nominee
12. Account with the Department of Agriculture in the name of a public entity (such as a state or local government, school district, or prison) that receives agricultural program payments	The public entity

[1] List first and circle the name of the person whose number you furnish. If only one person on a joint account has an SSN, that person's number must be furnished.

[2] Circle the minor's name and furnish the minor's SSN.

[3] You must show your individual name and you may also enter your business or "DBA" name on the second name line. You may use either your SSN or EIN (if you have one). If you are a sole proprietor, IRS encourages you to use your SSN.

[4] List first and circle the name of the legal trust, estate, or pension trust. (Do not furnish the TIN of the personal representative or trustee unless the legal entity itself is not designated in the account title.) Also see *Special rules regarding partnerships* on page 1.

Note. If no name is circled when more than one name is listed, the number will be considered to be that of the first name listed.

Privacy Act Notice

Section 6109 of the Internal Revenue Code requires you to provide your correct TIN to persons who must file information returns with the IRS to report interest, dividends, and certain other income paid to you, mortgage interest you paid, the acquisition or abandonment of secured property, cancellation of debt, or contributions you made to an IRA, or Archer MSA or HSA. The IRS uses the numbers for identification purposes and to help verify the accuracy of your tax return. The IRS may also provide this information to the Department of Justice for civil and criminal litigation, and to cities, states, the District of Columbia, and U.S. possessions to carry out their tax laws. We may also disclose this information to other countries under a tax treaty, to federal and state agencies to enforce federal nontax criminal laws, or to federal law enforcement and intelligence agencies to combat terrorism.

You must provide your TIN whether or not you are required to file a tax return. Payers must generally withhold 28% of taxable interest, dividend, and certain other payments to a payee who does not give a TIN to a payer. Certain penalties may also apply.

Figure 5.5 | Exhibit C

EXHIBIT C

<u>Replacement Property Identification Form</u>

The undersigned Transferor has entered into an Exchange Agreement ("Exchange Agreement") with Investors Title Exchange Corporation ("ITEC"), which contemplates a tax-deferred exchange of real property. Transferor understands that the Replacement Property must be identified either by: (i) street address, city and state; or (ii) legal description, within the period beginning on the date of the transfer of the first Relinquished Property and ending on midnight of the 45th calendar day thereafter.

Transferor understands that they may identify up to three replacement properties without regard to fair market value. However, if more than three properties are identified, the total, combined fair market value of all identified properties may not exceed 200% of the fair market value of the relinquished property. If Transferor intends to acquire an undivided interest in the replacement property, rather than a 100% interest in the property, Transferor shall identify the percentage of interest in the property it intends to acquire. Transferors shall consult their tax counsel if they have any questions regarding property identification of the replacement property.

In accordance with the Exchange Agreement and Section 1031 of the Tax Code and the pertinent Treasury Regulations promulgated thereunder, Transferor hereby identifies the following property as Replacement Property:

1)

2)

3)

_____ Additional space is required, so a separate sheet is attached hereto.

Transferor understands that if they do not ultimately acquire the Replacement Property by the earlier of (I) 180 calendar days from the date of the transfer of the first relinquished property, or (ii) the due date of its federal tax return for the year in which the closing on the Relinquished Property occurred, the exchange contemplated by the Exchange Agreement may be taxable. Further, Transferor understands that the Exchange Balance may only be used to acquire identified Replacement Property within the 180-day Exchange Period.

Executed on this _____ day of _____, 20____.

TRANSFEROR:

By:_____
    NAME

By:_____
    NAME

This document may be sent by facsimile to ITEC using the following number: (919) 968-2225.

© Investors Title Exchange Corporation. Reprinted with permission for illustration purposes only.
www.1031itec.com

Figure 5.6 | Relinquished Property Assignment

RELINQUISHED PROPERTY ASSIGNMENT
(Brief Property Description)

THIS RELINQUISHED PROPERTY ASSIGNMENT is made, by and between
_____ ("Transferor"); Investors Title Exchange Corporation ("ITEC"); and
_____ ("Purchaser");

Transferor and Purchaser entered into a Purchase and Sale Agreement dated
_____ (the "Contract"), which contract is incorporated by reference herein, whereby
Transferor agreed to sell certain real property described in the Contract (the "Relinquished
Property"). Transferor wishes to assign its interest in the Contract to sell the Relinquished
Property to ITEC in order to facilitate a tax-deferred exchange pursuant to Section 1031 of the
Internal Revenue Code.

NOW THEREFORE, for good and valuable consideration, the receipt and sufficiency of
which is hereby acknowledged, Transferor hereby assigns to ITEC all of Transferor's right, title and
interest in and to the Contract as to the sale of the Relinquished Property, and ITEC hereby accepts the
assignment. Notwithstanding the foregoing, Transferor shall remain solely liable to Purchaser
regarding any and all indemnities, representations and warranties contained in the Contract and ITEC
directs Transferor to transfer title to the Relinquished Property directly to Purchaser.

The undersigned Purchaser consents to this assignment and, notwithstanding such assignment,
the Purchaser agrees (i) to seek any remedy regarding a breach of any representation or warranty in the
Contract only against Transferor, and (ii) to enforce any and all indemnities in the Contract only against
Transferor and not against ITEC.

TRANSFEROR: _____ Date: _____

_____ Date: _____

ITEC: Investors Title Exchange Corporation

By: _____ Date: _____
Name:
Title:

PURCHASER: _____ Date: _____

_____ Date: _____

Figure 5.7 | Replacement Property Assignment

REPLACEMENT PROPERTY ASSIGNMENT
(Brief Property Description)

THIS REPLACEMENT PROPERTY ASSIGNMENT is made by and between
_____ ("Transferor"); Investors Title Exchange Corporation ("ITEC"); and
_____ ("Seller");

Transferor and Seller entered into a Purchase and Sale Agreement dated _____ (the "Contract"), which Contract is incorporated by reference herein, whereby Transferor agreed to purchase certain real property described in the Contract (the "Replacement Property"). Transferor wishes to assign Transferor's interest in the Contract to purchase the Replacement Property to ITEC in order to facilitate a tax-deferred exchange pursuant to Section 1031 of the Internal Revenue Code.

NOW THEREFORE, for good and valuable consideration, the receipt and sufficiency of which is hereby acknowledged, Transferor hereby assigns to ITEC all of Transferor's right, title and interest in and to the Contract and ITEC hereby accepts the assignment. Notwithstanding the foregoing, Transferor shall remain solely liable to Seller regarding any and all indemnities, representations and warranties contained in the Contract and ITEC directs Seller to transfer title to the Replacement Property directly to Transferor.

Any financial obligation to be assumed or entered into at closing shall be Transferor's responsibility solely, and Transferor shall be responsible for all costs of the acquisition of the Replacement Property pursuant to the Contract that exceed the amount of the Exchange Balance held by ITEC.

The undersigned Seller consents to this assignment and, notwithstanding such assignment, Seller agrees (i) to seek any remedy regarding a breach of any representations and warranties in the Contract only against Transferor; and (ii) to enforce any indemnities in the Contract only against Transferor and not against ITEC.

TRANSFEROR: _____   Date: _____

_____   Date: _____

ITEC: Investors Title Exchange Corporation

By:_____   Date_____
Name:
Title:

SELLER: _____   Date: _____

_____   Date: _____

Figure 5.8 | Addendum to Relinquished Property Statement

ADDENDUM TO RELINQUISHED PROPERTY CLOSING STATEMENT

Internal Revenue Code Section 1031 Exchange

The rights of the Seller in the Contract to which this Closing Statement relates have been previously assigned to Investors Title Exchange Corporation as a qualified intermediary in a tax-deferred exchange pursuant to Section 1031 of the Internal Revenue Code. As Assignee, Investors Title Exchange Corporation joins herein for the limited purpose of acknowledging that the net proceeds shown as payable to Seller on the face of the Closing Statement shall be received directly by Investors Title Exchange Corporation as the Assignee and as Intermediary, and thereafter held pursuant to an Exchange Agreement. References to the Seller on the face of the Closing Statement are for convenience of reference, it being understood and agreed that Investors Title Exchange Corporation is the seller in accordance with and by virtue of the prior assignment.

SELLER: _____

_____

INTERMEDIARY: INVESTORS TITLE EXCHANGE CORPORATION

By:_____
Name:
Title:

PURCHASER: _____

_____

Figure 5.9 | Computing the Capital Gain and Tax Due

	EXAMPLE	YOUR FIGURES
Step 1:		
Original Cost Basis (purchase price)	$100,000	$_____
+ Cost to Purchase (closing costs)	2,000	$_____
+ Capital Improvements	20,000	$_____
− Depreciation Taken (if any)	14,000	$_____
= Adjusted Cost Basis	$108,000	$_____
Step 2:		
Actual Sales Price	$324,000	$_____
− Cost to Sell (closing costs)	28,000	$_____
= Adjusted Sales Price	$296,000	$_____
Step 3:		
Adjusted Sales Price	$296,000	$_____
− Adjusted Cost Basis	108,000	$_____
= Capital Gain (or Loss)	$188,000	$_____
COMPUTING CAPITAL GAIN TAX		
Total Capital Gain (1)	$188,000	$_____
− Depreciation Taken (2)	14,000	$_____
= Appreciated Capital Gain (3)	$174,000	$_____
Appreciated Capital Gain × 15% = (4)	$26,100	$_____
− Depreciation Taken × 25% = (5)	3,500	$_____
Capital Gain Tax Due = (4) + (5)	$29,600	$_____

This is not an IRS form and should not be submitted to the IRS. The "Tax Due" is only an approximation of the tax due on the sale of the property. The actual "Tax Due" may be higher or lower depending on the balance of your tax return. It is strongly suggested that you seek the advice of a tax professional to determine an estimated tax due based on all your income and deductions. Estimated tax payments may be necessary to avoid underpayment penalties.

Frequently Asked Questions

Q. May a taxpayer exchange stock for stock?

A. Stock was specifically excluded from the 1031 law.

Q. May the sale of standing timber qualify for a 1031 tax-free exchange?

A. It may not qualify as real estate in spite of some state laws defining timber as real estate. Timber might possibly qualify in a personal property exchange if the taxpayer received personal property of the same class (lumber).

Q. May a taxpayer sell investment property and purchase a retirement home for himself or herself?

A. No, but the taxpayer would be allowed to purchase an investment home suitable for future occupancy as a retirement home (suggest taxpayer wait more than three years). The taxpayer must plan ahead.

Q. Is a "dealer" prohibited from executing a tax-free exchange?

A. A dealer is prohibited on a "dealer's" inventory property and principal residence. A dealer is not prohibited on a "dealer's" investment property and property held in the productive use in trade or business.

Q. May a taxpayer execute more than one tax-free exchange per year?

A. Yes.

Q. May a taxpayer use the same "safe harbor" more than once in the same year?

A. If the "safe harbor" was not a "disqualified person" on the first exchange, the "safe harbor" is qualified for all subsequent exchanges in that year or future years.

Q. Is there any way to acquire additional time to complete the exchange if one cannot close before the 180th day?

A. No.

Q. Once possible replacement properties have been identified may the list be altered (added to or deleted from)?

A. Yes, if the alteration is completed before the end of the 45th day.

Q. After the 45th day the *identified* list of properties may not be changed.

A. Correct; moreover, the three-property, 200 percent, and 95 percent rules go into effect.

■ Case Studies

Chapter One: General Discussion of Taxes

1. d.   Gain on the immediate sale of 427 Viking Way would be taxed as a short-term capital gain, rather than as a long-term capital gain.

2. a. $400,000. ($250,000 + $5,000 + $115,000 + $30,000 = $400,000; $959,000 – $400,000 = $559,000)

Chapter Two: Installment Sales

1. c.   Moira would not be responsible for maintenance and repairs in an installment sale.

2. d.   Her capital gains tax is spread out over the term of the seller financing.

Chapter Three: The 1031 Tax-Free Exchange

1. b.   The strip mall in Boulder is eligible. All other properties are ineligible.

2. c.   A 1031 exchange between Lorenzo and Michelle would be based on the equity.

Chapter Four: The Law and the Rules

A

1. a.   Real estate property must be exchanged for real estate property.

2. c.   To conduct a 100 percent tax-free 1031 exchange, Butch must buy up, mortgage up, and spend all the money.

B

1. d.   The taxpayer may not be in either actual or constructive receipt of the money.

2. a.   A qualified intermediary is the most common type of safe harbor.

■ Chapter Review Questions

Chapter One Review Answers

1. d.   Relinquished is the old property the taxpayer wishes to sell.
2. c.   Capital gain income is taxed lower than ordinary income.
3. a.   Replacement is the property the taxpayer will acquire in an exchange.

4. a. $1,487,500 − $237,000 = $1,250,500

5. b. $205,000 + $9,000 − $83,000 = $131,000

6. a. $487,000 − $37,000 = $450,000

7. c. $872,000 − $146,500 = $725,500

8. a. $478,000 − $146,000 = $332,000; $146,000 × 25% = $36,500; $332,000 × 15% = $49,800; $49,800 + $36,500 = $86,300

9. d. $206,000 × 25% = $51,500

10. c. $854,000 − $206,000 = $648,000; $648,000 × 15% = $97,200; $97,200 + $51,500 = $148,700

Chapter Two Review Answers

1. b.   After closing, the buyer is responsible for maintenance of the property.

2. b.   There are always risks associated with almost any business transaction.

3. a.   The buyer and seller negotiate all terms such as interest rate, duration of loan, and frequency of payments on an installment sale.

4. b.   Installment sales can close very quickly.

5. b. $135,000 × 15% = $20,250; $45,000 × 15% = $6,750; $20,250 − $6,750 = $13,500.

6. d.   The cost basis is never taxed.

7. b.   The depreciated capital gain is recaptured at 25 percent.

8. c.   The interest portion of an installment payment is taxed at the taxpayer's income tax rate.

9. a.   The appreciated capital gain portion of an installment payment is taxed at 15 percent.

10. d. $1,200 × 12 = $14,400; $14,400 − $3,800 = $10,600; $10,600 × 15% = $1,590.

Chapter Three Review Answers

1. a.   *Deferred* is the word associated with Thomas J. Starker.

2. b.   A taxpayer may not exchange a second home.

3. b.   No, this real estate is the inventory property of builder Minton. Inventory property is not eligible for exchanges.

4. d.   By buying up, mortgaging up, and spending all the money, the taxpayer would have executed a 100 percent tax-free exchange.

5. a.   Boot is taxable to the recipient in the year received, not the year "earned."

6. b.   The first acknowledged exchanges were in the 1920s.

7. b. $125,000 − $80,000 = $45,000.

8. c.   Equity is the basis of an exchange.

9. a.   *Unlike-kind* property is another phrase for boot.

10. c. $350,000 − $87,000 − $28,000 = $235,000 cash proceeds. Only sale c buys up, mortgages up, and spends all the money.

Chapter Four Review Answers

1. b.   Exchanges must be finalized within 180 days from the closing (sale) of the relinquished property.

2. a.   This is one of the requirements of Section 1031 of the Internal Revenue Code.

3. d.   This is an attempt to exchange real estate for a NASCAR racing car. They are not "like kind."

4. d.   *Identification* must be accomplished within 45 days of the closing of the relinquished property.

5. b.   Foreign exchanges can be accomplished.

6. b.   The taxpayer may exchange a truck for a truck or a copying machine for a copying machine but not a truck for a copying machine.

7. b.   The taxpayer is not allowed to be in actual or constructive receipt of any of the proceeds of sale until after all replacement properties are acquired and the exchange period (180 days) has expired.

8. b.   Leases for more than 30 years qualify for 1031 treatment.

9. d.   Once the taxpayer identifies and buys more than three properties, their total purchase price may not exceed 200 percent of the sales price of the relinquished property.

10. a.   An unlimited number and dollar amount of replacement properties may be purchased if accomplished within the 45 days. *Identification* rules do not apply if you do not *identify*.

Chapter Five Review Answers

1. c.   The seller and safe harbor sign the exchange agreement. The buyer has nothing to do with it.

2. a.   This is true. See assignment forms for relinquished and replacement properties.

3. d.   The sales contract is where the buyer and seller agree that the taxpayer has the right to assign his or her interests under that contract to his or her safe harbor.

4. b.   The opposite is true. The exchange agreement specifically says that the safe harbor has no liability for the property condition.

5. b.   The sales contract is the only possible answer that is not a part of the exchange agreement.

accelerated depreciation A method of depreciation whereby the taxpayer could take depreciation above the straight-line method, thus creating an additional tax shelter for the taxpayer. The 1997 Tax Reform Act eliminated accelerated depreciation.

adjusted cost basis The purchase price plus the buyer's closing costs plus the improvements, minus any depreciation taken.

adjusted sales price The sales price minus the seller's closing costs.

appreciated capital gain The portion of the capital gain associated with the increase in value of the asset during ownership. Appreciated capital gains are presently taxed at a maximum of 15 percent.

boot Anything received in an exchange that is not "like kind." In a real estate exchange, the receipt of cash or anything other than real estate is *boot*, including a reduction in mortgage indebtedness. Boot is also called *unlike-kind property* and is always taxable to the recipient.

capital gains A tax resulting from the sale of a capital asset at a price higher than the purchase price. Capital gains occur when the adjusted sales price is higher than the adjusted cost basis.

capital loss A tax deduction resulting from the sale of a capital asset at a price lower than the purchase price. Capital loss occurs when the adjusted cost basis is greater than the adjusted sales price. A capital loss cannot be claimed for assets used personally by the taxpayer and is limited to $3,000 per year.

dealer A person whose ordinary income is derived from activities that would result in capital gain income for most taxpayers. Examples: car dealers, real estate developers.

depreciated capital gain The portion of the capital gain associated with the depreciation taken by a taxpayer during the time of ownership. It will be taxed at 15/25 percent. This is called *recapture.*

depreciation The loss in value over time of improvements to real estate. While an investment property may be appreciating in value, an owner may depreciate the property for tax purposes. Depreciation may be used to offset income of investment property. A taxpayer's principal resi-dence may not be depreciated. Land may not be depreciated.

held A word used twice in the 1031 law to indicate that the taxpayer wishing to exchange must hold (have title and all rights and responsibilities incident to ownership) the relinquished property and replacement property.

installment sale A method of selling an asset that the seller financed with interest on the sale of his or her real estate; the capital gains tax is spread out over a number of years. Installment sale is also known as *owner-financing* or *seller-financing.*

interest Anything paid as compensation for the use of money. Examples: mortgage interest, car loan interest, interest paid to the IRS for delinquent taxes.

like-kind One of the requirements of a 1031 tax-free exchange is that the properties must be like kind. *Like-kind* means that real estate held for the productive use in trade, business, or investment property must be exchanged for property held for the productive use in trade, business, or investment property.

long-term capital gain An asset held for more than one year and then sold will be taxed at a lower rate than property held for less than one year. The highest rate is 15 percent for most taxpayers. For taxpayers in the lowest two tax brackets (presently 10 percent and 15 percent) the rate is 5 percent.

qualified intermediary One of the four types of safe harbors. An entity created to satisfy the tax-free exchange laws that require the taxpayer not to be in actual or constructive receipt of the proceeds of sale of the relinquished property.

recapture Upon the sale of investment property the IRS collects a 15 or 25 percent tax on the amount of depreciation taken by the taxpayer during the period of ownership. (It is more an action by IRS than a name.)

related exchange An exchange whereby the taxpayer is "related" to another party in the exchange by blood or marriage or to a partnership or corporation in which the taxpayer has a significant interest.

relinquished property The "old" property that a taxpayer wishes to sell as part of a tax-free exchange.

replacement property   The "new" property that a taxpayer wishes to acquire as part of a tax-free exchange.

safe harbor   A broad term to describe those places where the proceeds of the sale of a taxpayer's real estate may be placed to ensure that the taxpayer is not in actual or constructive receipt of those proceeds. The qualified intermediary is the most frequently used type of safe harbor.

short-term capital gain   An asset held for one year or less and then sold is treated as ordinary income. The taxpayer may pay taxes on the short-term capital gain at his or her tax bracket, possibly as high as 35 percent.

straight-line depreciation   The basic method of calculating depreciation on real estate. The 1986 Tax Reform Act made this the only method allowed (eliminating the accelerated depreciation methods for real estate). It is computed by taking the purchase price minus the land value divided by 27.5 for residential property and divided by 39 for nonresidential property. This figure is be used as the amount of depreciation that may be taken each year until fully depreciated.

tax-free exchange   A strategy for selling investment property to defer the normal capital gains tax until some future time by selling the relinquished property and acquiring the replacement property according to the rules found in Section 1031 of the U.S. Internal Revenue Code. Also called *tax-deferred exchange, like-kind exchange, Starker deferred exchange, 1031 exchange,* and *Starker exchange.*